DUE   DATE RET

First Intermissions

First
Intermissions

Twenty–One Great Operas
Explored, Explained, and Brought to Life
From the Met

M. OWEN LEE

New York   Oxford

OXFORD UNIVERSITY PRESS   1995

OXFORD UNIVERSITY PRESS

Oxford   Calcutta   Madras   Karachi
Kuala Lumpur   Singapore   New York   Toronto
Delhi   Bombay   Hong Kong   Tokyo
Nairobi   Del es Salaam   Cape Town
Melbourne   Auckland   Madrid

and associated companies in
Berlin   Ibadan

Published by Oxford University Press, Inc.,
200 Madison Avenue, New York, New York 10016

Oxford is a registered trademark of Oxford University Press

Library of Congress Cataloging-in-Publication Data
Lee, M. Owen, 1930–
First intermissions : twenty-one great operas explored,
explained, and brought to life from the Met / M. Owen Lee.
p. cm.   Based on the author's intermission commentaries from
Metropolitan Opera radio broadcasts.
Includes bibliographical references and index.
ISBN 0-19-509255-4
1. Operas—Analysis, appreciation.   I. Title.
MT95.L514   1995   782.1′015—dc20   94-10113

3 5 7 9 8 6 4 2

Printed in the United States of America
on acid-free paper

FOR

RICHARD MOHR

Preface

Ideally, each of these commentaries should be read during the first intermission of the opera it discusses because it was for the first intermissions of the Saturday afternoon Metropolitan Opera broadcasts that each was originally conceived, and it was over the Texaco Radio Network that they were heard by an audience of, on at least some Saturdays, eight million or more people.

Many from the radio audience have asked, in letters through the years, for this volume. I sometimes think that their letters would make a more interesting volume than the one they asked for. When I spoke on *Les Troyens* (my heart-in-throat debut on the first intermissions), I received a grateful response from a third-generation descendant of Heinrich Schliemann, the famous archaeologist who first excavated Homer's Troy, and another from a university professor of English who remembered walking Homer's Troy by moonlight, "listening to the wind in the pines and the waves of the Aegean lapping the shore."

My intermission commentary on *Turandot* was controversial, with mail running only about seven to one in favor of what I said; some of those who disagreed were (perhaps justifiably) enraged. Opera lovers are a passionate lot. My venturesome but hardly unorthodox ideas on *Lohengrin* brought perhaps the most favorable mail, but also three angry letters from three different religious perspectives. (One of the three wrote eloquently later to clarify and soften her initial response.)

The most widely divergent responses came after I spoke on *Parsifal,* though the hundred or more letters were, this time, uniformly positive responses: Wagnerians said that I had stated for them the essence of Wagner's meaning; anti-Wagnerians said that I had made them surrender at last to the composer's spell; religious people told me I had strengthened their faith; Jungians thanked me for explaining the archetypes; and a practicing therapist, to my astonishment, declared that he had never heard schizophrenia so clearly elucidated. It was a demonstration of how opera can mean many things, and true things, to many different people. *Parsifal* is perhaps the most controversial of all operas, and yet the letters I received said over and over that Wagner's last opera was what that eminent historian of medieval philosophy, Etienne Gilson, once told me it was: "the most beautiful of all operas, highest in the heaven of heavens."

Parsifal I was invited to comment on twice, during the first intermission of the opera itself, and during the last intermission the previous week, when the opera was Verdi's *Don Carlo.* That explains why the *Parsifal* chapter here is so long, and why it begins with a reference to Schiller. The idealistic German not only wrote the play on which Verdi's *Don Carlo* is based but also gave us the categories—*naiv* and *sentimentalisch*—most helpful for assessing the work of both the Maestro and the Meister. Schiller was my best defense for presuming to speak on a Wagner opera during a Verdi intermission.

The long chapter on *Die Meistersinger* was, similarly, given in two parts, the first prepared at the last minute and given during an intermission of, again, a Verdi opera, *Ernani.* I hope that the great Italian has forgiven me for the Wagner intermissions I gave between the acts of two of his finest works. Late in life, he came to respect the German titan who was for so long his arch-rival.

The commentaries appear here in a form somewhat different from that in which they were heard live on the air. Last-minute cuts (and, *horresco referens,* last-minute additions) often had to be made in them at broadcast time. Most of the cuts have been restored here. On the other hand, the piano illustrations, so essential to radio commentaries accompanying live broadcasts, have been reduced here to the minimum essential to reading. And while my conversational style, with its dashes and its half-sentences, has been largely preserved, the occasional phrase has been altered to address not some eight million listeners during a first intermission but the reader with this volume in hand. Finally, the commentaries have been arranged in a sequence that will, I hope, enable them to be seen not as a collection of self-contained essays so much as a book to be read through, a volume that reflects one opera-lover's sensibility.

Mozart is underrepresented here. He wrote most of his operas in two acts, and on the Metropolitan broadcasts of those works the sole intermission is taken up, as is almost always the case with two-act operas, with that most popular of Texaco features, the Opera Quiz. But while I have spoken on Mozart to the radio audience only once (during the first intermission of the three-act *Idomeneo*), I nonetheless regard him, as most musicians do, as supreme among composers, and what I have to say about his *Don Giovanni* and *The Magic Flute,* as well as about Beethoven's *Fidelio,* is available in cassette form from the Metropolitan Opera Guild.

I would like to thank Texaco, for more than fifty years the sponsor of the Metropolitan Opera Broadcasts, for permission to reproduce my first intermissions here. Thanks are also due to the Metropolitan Opera Guild's magazine, *Opera News,* where some of my remarks on *Idomeneo, Rigoletto, Don Carlo,*

Faust, Hoffmann, Turandot, Rosenkavalier, and the Wagner operas first appeared; to the San Francisco Opera, whose magazine first printed some of my remarks on *Manon*; to *The Opera Quarterly*; to the editors of the *International Dictionary of Opera*; and to Leroy R. Shaw, the editor of *Wagner in Retrospect: A Centennial Reappraisal* (Amsterdam, 1987), where some of the material on *Die Meistersinger* also appeared. I am grateful to Hendon Music for permission to quote excerpts from the score of *Turandot,* and to Boosey & Hawkes and European American Music Distributors Corporation for permission to quote excerpts from the scores of *Elektra, Der Rosenkavalier,* and *Die Frau ohne Schatten.* I owe an immense debt to Maribeth Anderson Payne, Soo Mee Kwon, and Paul Schlotthauer at Oxford University Press, who had faith in this project and saw it to completion. My special thanks, too, for help given in various ways, to Edward Downes, James K. Farge, John B. Harcourt, Winnie Klotz, Charles Leland, Irene Sloan, and Vinnie Volpe.

But most of all I should like to thank the former producer of the broadcast intermissions, to whom this book is dedicated. His is one of the most important names in the history of opera on record. He produced the postwar RCA recordings of some fifty operas and of many instrumental works as well, and a fair number of those recordings still stand unchallenged today. He was for several years a panelist par excellence on the broadcast features before he became their producer, and for the past ten years he has been my mentor and stay during the first intermissions when with quaking fingers I dared illustrate at the keyboard the storm off the coast of Cyprus, the skyey vision of the Holy Grail, or the menacing shadow of Agamemnon's ghost on the wall of Mycenae. But I am most grateful to him for first having confidence in me when, as a Catholic priest with only a few years of piano lessons learned in depression Detroit from the Sisters of Charity, I must have seemed the most unlikely of all intermission possibilities.

On the intermissions themselves, his instructions were simple: I could say anything I pleased so long as (1) it was instantly intelligible to the little old lady in Dubuque and the little old gentleman in Des Moines, and (2) it was something no one anywhere, of either sex or any age, had ever thought of before. I hope, then, that all of what follows is intelligible, and that at least some of it you, gentle reader, have never thought of before and will, on reading, find convincing and true.

Toronto   M. O. L.
April 1994

Contents

First Intermissions

Idomeneo
Courtesy Winnie Klotz, Photographer
Metropolitan Opera Association Inc.

A
NEW KIND
OF OPERA

Idomeneo

I first came in contact with the figure of King Idomeneo not through Mozart's opera but through Homer's *Iliad*. In that oldest epic of the Western world, Idomeneus, as he is called in Greek, brings one of the largest fighting contingents to the Trojan War. He leads eighty of the thousand ships launched by Helen's beautiful face. He is only a supporting actor in the story and, while not so old as old Nestor, he is less youthful than the other Greeks at Troy. He's a good fighter though, and because he rules over that great sea power Crete, the sea god comes to watch him when he fights. His big moment occurs in Book XIII of the *Iliad,* when he comes face to face in battle with Trojan Aeneas, and stands up to him like a mountain boar, with bristling back and flaming eyes.

But, strangely, Homer tells us nothing of the story we get in Mozart's opera—how the same King Idomeneus was caught in a storm sailing home and vowed to the sea god that, if saved, he would sacrifice the first living creature he saw on shore, and then found, by a terrible twist of fate, that the victim he had to sacrifice was his own son.

5

That story doesn't crop up among the legends of Homer's Idomeneus for another ten centuries. We don't hear of it until the Romans write commentaries on Virgil's *Aeneid*. But it's a story that was bound to make its way sooner or later into the Greek hero-myth because it is, to use the technical term, archetypal. It's a story told by all races and tribes. It is told, in only slightly different form, in the Bible—where Abraham is called on by God to sacrifice his only son, who is saved at the last minute, and where Jephthah, after a hasty vow, actually does sacrifice his only daughter. There are traces of the story in the Greek myths of Agamemnon's sacrificing his daughter Iphigeneia and of Meander's sacrificing his son, and in the myths of many other civilizations. Some stories are so archetypal, so emblematic of the conflicts in our lives, that all races and cultures *have* to tell them.

Probably no story in the Western tradition has been told so often as that vast, burgeoning story of the Trojan War. It gave birth to countless poems and dramas in the ancient world— and how many operas? Once, on the Opera Quiz, I easily strung together ten Trojan War operas in sequence. But that was nothing. A recent German study lists, for the seventeenth century alone, a full thirty-seven operas on Helen of Troy, and fifty-three more on Agamemnon, fifty-two on Achilles, fifty-seven on Odysseus, thirty-three on Aeneas, and ninety-six on Dido—and those are just some of the main figures connected with the Trojan War.

Most of those operas are lost to us now. They were all specimens of that seventeeth-century kind of opera called *opera seria*. Mozart's *Idomeneo* is probably the greatest *opera seria* ever written. It is also one of the last. It is *opera seria* in the process of becoming something new, something closer to opera as we know it today. In *Idomeneo* Mozart is changing everything. No *opera seria,* till this one, had music in it like this—music that looks not backward to the baroque but forward to romanticism:

That sounds like Beethoven and his piano sonatas, but it's actually Mozart a generation earlier, in *Idomeneo*'s last act, challenging and changing the opera of the past.

Opera seria held the stage from about 1650 to 1750, and it was as much an industry as is today's film industry. Each passing year would bring hundreds of new operas. But there was a sameness about them: they dealt almost exclusively with Greek and Roman subjects. And though the composer might be a German, like Handel, writing for Englishmen, Italian was always the favored language. Stranger still, many of the leading roles were sung by castrati, male sopranos and altos. The *opere serie* ought to have been exciting pieces (some of the composers were great composers, and the mythological subjects featured such potential for excitement as monsters and battles and floods), but tradition dictated that the music be a stately succession of long arias separated by longer stretches of recitative, while the drama inched its way toward an inevitable happy ending designed to show the wisdom and clemency of the ruler for whom the opera was commissioned. No wonder, with political revolution in the eighteenth-century air, *opera seria* was on the way out!

Mozart was twenty-four when the commission came from Munich to write an *opera seria* for the beautiful little Cuvilliés Theater there, and the installation of the elector, Karl Theodor. Mozart was a young man eager to prove himself, eager to innovate, and here at last was the chance. His wife, Constanze, said later that this was the happiest time of his life, and *Idomeneo* was, we know from Mozart's own letters, the work he loved most of all his operas—perhaps because, after a decade of being idolized as a child prodigy and then another decade of being studiously ignored, he emerged in this opera as a mature man and a composer of genius. He was ready to make important changes.

He thought that his genius was most evident in the quartet "Andrò ramingo e solo" in the last act. Instead of the four long arias that, say, Handel would have given us, we hear, simultaneously, four voices blended, four characters in four different moods singing simultaneously: Idomeneo in despair over his rash vow; Idamante resolved to prove his manhood; Ilia comforting them both; and Elettra tormented by jealousy. Though there are similarly complex pages in Scarlatti and a few earlier composers, Mozart's is by common consent the first great ensemble in opera, a forerunner of the trio in *Der Rosenkavalier,* the quartet in *Rigoletto,* the quintet in *Die Meistersinger.*

The other advances Mozart made in *Idomeneo,* over a century of earlier *opere serie,* are—I should say—three. First there is a new musical continuity. Previous operas had been rigidly sectioned off into arias in which the soloists were given ample opportunity for vocal display and even more ample opportunity to acknowledge applause. In *Idomeneo,* the first aria melts into the following recitative, even as the overture had melted easily into it. This is an anticipation of the techniques of Wagner, but that apostle of musical continuity was well into his forties when he decided that this was the right way to write overture and aria. Mozart knew as much early in his twenties.

The most famous of the Wagnerian methods of continuity is the leitmotif: the short recurrent theme that carries reminiscences and new implications with every new appearance. But a hundred years before Wagner's *Tristan,* Mozart, in *Idomeneo,* experimented with something quite similar, our second new advance over earlier operatic writing: the brief, recurrent phrase pervading the score, changing its form, instrumentation, harmonization, and rhythm as it develops its ever-new associations. On the first page of the overture we hear one of these. It is a five-note descending figure:

It soon comes to dominate the overture, depicting the *Sturm und Drang,* the storm and stress of the sea-music. A few pages later, it reappears in the recitative, as Ilia remembers the fall of Troy, and it appears again in the accompaniment to the aria that follows. Then when Ilia's beloved, Idamante, tells her that he will make her forget her past sufferings, it appears again, much brighter in color. It recurs quietly when King Idomeneo comes safely to land, and a moment later it accompanies his realization that now he will have to keep his vow to the sea god, and sacrifice to him the first living thing he finds on shore. It recurs once again when he looks fatefully on that victim, his own son, and the son doesn't understand why his father tears himself away from his embrace.

The English critic David Cairns has suggested that by this time the theme has come to bear associations both of nature's cruelty and of our own inner sufferings. In Act II it forms part of the musical line of the powerful aria "Fuor del mar," where Idomeneo sings of both the storm at sea and the storm within himself. It then hovers over the little duet of the two lovers in Act III. And it reappears when Idomeneo finally tells his subjects that he must sacrifice his own son. There it leads to a passage of more chromatic intensity than anyone had ever heard in an opera house before.

And finally, our melodic fragment leads gently into the last recitative, when Idomeneo turns over the kingdom to his son. There it is stated four times over, canonically, by the four separate string sections of the orchestra.

A third new element in *Idomeneo* is the wholly unprecedented attention to orchestral color. The young Mozart was excited that the finest orchestra in the world, the Mannheim ensemble, was following the elector to Munich for the premiere. It was a virtuoso ensemble. According to a description of the day, "Its piano was a vernal breath, its forte was thunder, its crescendo a cataract, its diminuendo a crystal stream murmuring as it evanesced into the distance." All of those effects Mozart wrote into *Idomeneo,* using muted tympani, muted trumpets, and massed trombones. The sea that surges and foams around the island of Crete is suggested, in the overture and the storm music, by swirling strings. The color conjured up in those passages is, for me, a kind of grayish green. But many more colors are suggested throughout the opera, especially by the woodwind writing. This was virtuoso music for its day, and music of a wholly new loveliness.

Ten years after *Idomeneo,* in the last months of his life, Mozart wrote one last *opera seria—La Clemenza di Tito,* a piece admired by Goethe and Kleist, a piece that inspired Shelley to write the poem that begins, "I arise from dreams of thee." Then, for more than a century, *Idomeneo* and *Clemenza* were forgotten by the world's opera houses—because in between *Idomeneo* and *Clemenza* Mozart, always experimenting, had changed the course of opera. Instead of refashioning the old form of *opera seria,* he chose, in his other works for the stage, to blend *opera seria* with the newer *opera buffa,* to juxtapose the serious and the comic. So those wonderful seriocomedies, *Le Nozze di Figaro, Don Giovanni, Così Fan Tutte,* and *The Magic Flute* made their way around the world, and Mozart's two wholly "serious operas," his *opere serie,* went completely out of fashion.

Until these past few decades. Now *Idomeneo* and *Clemenza* are holding the stage once more. And I'm happy to say that it was the most famous of commentators on these first intermissions, Boris Goldovsky, who led the first staged performances of *Idomeneo* in this country, at the Berkshire Festival in 1947, almost two centuries after the Munich premiere. Those Goldovsky performances heralded the re-emergence in America of Mozart as an *opera seria* composer. *Idomeneo*, we now can see, is not an opera hopelessly out of date but an opera for all seasons, for all times and places. I'd like, finally, to illustrate that.

At the end of his book *In Defense of Opera*, Hamish Swanston tells the true story of an African bodyguard, a giant of a man recruited to accompany the president of a developing country to a conference in Geneva. The African knocked at midnight on the door of a Swiss professor of law to ask what "that wonderful music" was, playing on the gramophone. He stayed to listen to the professor's recording through the night, and then eventually took it back with him to his village. The music that bridged the culture gap that night was *Idomeneo*. The piece that spoke with directness to the African was a piece that the theaters of Europe and America had laid aside for some two hundred years, so tenacious was the idea on those continents that *opera seria* was dead. The African instinctively knew better.

Maybe, more in touch with myth and its wonders, he could hear in the music something we missed over two centuries. This story of a father called to sacrifice his own child is both timeless, told of those archetypal fathers in Greek myth and the Bible, and—perhaps in this quarter-hour I haven't said enough about this—it was also a story intensely personal to the young man who wrote the music. Mozart knew, in composing it, that he was no longer a child prodigy but a man of genius. His father was soon, like Idomeneo, to relinquish his stern control over his life. And he himself, like Idamante, would come into his kingdom, into the fullness of his powers.

The breakthrough work for Wolfgang Amadeus Mozart was *Idomeneo*. It told one of our great archetypal stories, and it was, at least partly, about Mozart himself.

No wonder it is full of wonderful music.

Aida
Courtesy Winnie Klotz, Photographer
Metropolitan Opera Association Inc.

WHEN
VERDI'S FATHERS
SING

Rigoletto

There is at least one moment in every Verdi opera when you can almost palpably sense the effect of the music on the audience. I think it is something only Verdi of all composers can command. At that moment the audience is moved not to applaud but to catch its breath. For what it responds to is not some climactic high note, nor some orchestral peroration, but a sudden outpouring of melody—direct, honest, intense, and unashamed. At that moment, be the opera as familiar as *Aida* or as unfamiliar as *Alzira,* you are one with the characters on stage. You say to yourself, "Yes, I have felt that too, in my life. Verdi has read my heart."

I first saw Verdi's opera *The Sicilian Vespers* in Germany under less than favorable circumstances. I had no opportunity to read any synopsis of the plot beforehand. I bought a low-priced ticket and hurried to my place (high in the gallery, the last seat over to the side) within minutes of starting time. When the curtain rose I saw less than one-third of the stage. The opera was done not in French, as Verdi first wrote it, or

15

in Italian, which is the language in which it is most often heard, but in strange-sounding German, and it was rather indifferently performed. All the same, Verdi's music was soon sweeping all before it.

Five-act operas are often performed with only one intermission in Germany, and so I still had no precise idea of the plot when we arrived without a break at the scene in the middle of the opera where the powerful old French governor was alone in his study reading a letter, from which it was suddenly clear to him and, as suddenly, to me that the rebellious young Italian who hated him so much was actually his own son. The music in which the father voiced his feelings for the son he had never known began to touch me deeply. Some time before, I had lost my own father.

Then the son was brought in, a captive, and the father asked for understanding, forgiveness, and affection—all of which the son denied him. Soon the two were launched into a passionate duet based on the big theme I had known for years from the opera's overture. The melody had meant nothing to me before, but now, heard in its context, as a father used it to plead with his son, I felt a flood of emotion, the feelings any son might have when suddenly, powerfully reminded of his dead father—the memory of disagreements, of failed opportunities, of a mutual inability to express tenderness, and above all the regret that it was now too late to make amends. It was all there, in the music. Verdi had read my heart.

In virtually every opera by Verdi something like that will happen. And in virtually every opera by Verdi the same figure commands the stage: the father passionately devoted to and often in conflict with his children. The very first duet Verdi wrote, in *Oberto,* is a long reconciliation scene between a father and a daughter, a scene he recreated masterfully some forty years later in the revision of *Simon Boccanegra.* And between

those two works there is a whole gallery of passionate, eloquent, often self-contradictory father figures.

In *Nabucco* an Old Testament king is rejected by his adopted
daughter and loved by the daughter who is his own flesh and
blood, though he understands their true feelings only when it
is too late. In *I Masnadieri* a German count is left to die by the
son he had thought faithful, rescued by the son he had thought
hated him. In *I Due Foscari* a Venetian doge is forced by his
council to send his last surviving son into exile, and the son—
innocent of the charge against him—says farewell to his two
small boys. In *La Battaglia di Legnano* a Milanese soldier embraces his little son as he leaves for battle, and asks that the
boy be brought up to fear God and love his country above all
else. In *Macbeth* a Scottish soldier weeps that his innocent children have all been put to the sword when he was not there to
save them. In *Giovanna d'Arco* Joan of Arc's father comes to
understand her mission only after he has betrayed her and it is
too late to undo the wrong. In *Luisa Miller* two fathers, one
full of love and the other full of hate, watch unavailing as their
two children, who are in love, die together. In *La Traviata* a
father comes to love the woman whose heart he must break
more than the son for whose sake he intervenes; she becomes
a surrogate daughter to him. In *La Forza del Destino* a dying
father lays a curse on his daughter, and a kindly old priest becomes a second father for her. In *Don Carlo* a terrifying old
priest persuades a father to consign his son to death. In *Aida* a
father uses paternal tenderness and paternal threats to bend his
daughter to his will. And so it goes—in opera after opera by
Verdi, the father is powerful and ambivalent, and sons and
daughters sing "Padre, mio padre" in tenderness or in terror
or in tears.

Only when Verdi was an old patriarch himself, when he was
done adapting Schiller and Byron, Dumas and Victor Hugo,

when he was working exclusively with Shakespearian subjects, only then did he let the "padre," the "vecchio genitor," fade out of his work. His librettist Boito eliminated the fathers Brabantio and Page when he adapted Shakespeare's *Othello* and *The Merry Wives of Windsor.* Old Verdi did not insist on father figures any more. And he decided that he never would write the Shakespearian work he was moving toward all his life, the work that would surely have provided him with his greatest father, *King Lear.*

For the greatest Verdi father, then, we return to the middle of the composer's career, to the hunchback Rigoletto, a deeply ambivalent man who keeps just one part of his evil life pure— the part he reserves for his beloved daughter. Many listeners remember Rigoletto, as they remember Giorgio Germont in *La Traviata,* for his tenderness. Germont sings to Violetta, as if she were his daughter, "Piangi" ("Weep"):

Pian - gi,　　pian - gi,　　pian - gi, o ___ mi - se - ra.

And similarly Rigoletto sings to his Gilda, "Piangi" ("Weep"):

Pian - gi,　　pian - gi, fan-ciul - la, fan-ciul-la, pian - gi.

But these two fathers are not always so tender and sympathetic. (Neither is the marvelous, ambivalent mother figure Verdi gives us in that third midcareer masterpiece, *Il Trovatore.* They are complex figures, these Verdi parents.) Rigoletto is as full of hate as he is of love. That contradiction is what attracted

Verdi to him. When he found him in the pages of Victor Hugo, he thought the hunchback "worthy of Shakespeare." Worthy of Shakespeare is what, at least, the hunchback became in the pages of Verdi.

Rigoletto is not only outwardly deformed, so that he must limp and lurch about the stage. He is not just a jester with a tongue that lashes and cuts. He is inwardly as well as outwardly vile. He is an evil man. At the court of Mantua he has corrupted the young Duke, perverting his good instincts, pimping for him, pushing him further and further into vice, and hating him all the while. He even suggests that the Duke simply kill off any father or husband that stands in the way of his lust. Old Count Monterone is right, as he lays a father's curse on Rigoletto, to call him a dog, a serpent. Even the depraved courtiers want to destroy Rigoletto, for they have all felt his sting.

But, we note, the despicable Rigoletto is superior to the others in intelligence. He has an intellectual's antithetical cast of mind, as when he says of himself and the assassin he hires to kill the Duke, "I kill with the tongue, he with the knife." A man paid to make others laugh, he is not without wit in his grim antitheses. "He is crime," he says of the young Duke as he sets the trap for him, "I am punishment." And again, on the stormy night that witnesses the opera's final horrors, he observes, "Una tempesta in ciel, in terra un omicidio." ("A tempest in heaven, and on earth a murder.")

To the world Rigoletto appears to be utterly without feeling. Reflecting on his jester's state, he says bitterly, "I can't even weep, which is the refuge of other men." But later in the opera, when his public and private lives are thrown violently together, he will find much to weep over and—this is the measure of his stature as a character—we will find ourselves weeping with him. For as he once knew happiness with a woman who really loved him and then died young, so he has preserved in his heart one love that keeps him, in spite of all, a human being—his love for his daughter, Gilda.

Is there, then, a more pathetic moment in opera than the moment in the second act when, in the Duke's palace, Gilda exclaims, "Mio padre!" and sees him for the first time in his vulgar jester's costume, and he sees her in her ravished garments, and each, in a blinding moment, realizes what shame has been visited on the other? Is there a more horrific moment than the one in the last act, when Gilda exclaims again, "Mio padre!" and realizes, first, that her father is plotting a murder and, second, that he may soon be caught in his own trap and killed himself? Is there any more ironic moment than the last moment in the opera, when Rigoletto opens the assassin's sack and finds that the body within is not the Duke he hates but the daughter he loves? He shouts that he has been destroyed by the curse a father laid on him at the opera's start, but we who have seen his drama know that he has as surely been destroyed by the evil he has all along nursed within himself.

William Weaver, that connoisseur of all good things Italian, once said on the Metropolitan broadcasts that *Rigoletto* had the best libretto of any opera. It certainly has a libretto full of ironies and ambiguities at every turn. And, as George Bernard Shaw put it, the libretto was "burned into music by Verdi." We rightly love *Rigoletto* for its melodies, but Verdi would be disappointed in us if we didn't see those melodies as, above all, integral to the terrible, heartbreaking story. He fought fiercely with his censors to keep every detail of that story: the hump, the curse, the rape, the murder, and the sack. "It is precisely because of these that I chose the subject," he said. He knew that the story could wring from him music to move us all. He also knew that, in spite of or perhaps because of the grotesqueness, Rigoletto was a figure for any one of us. Writ large, of course, as a tragic figure must be. If, please God, no one of us has hated so much, neither perhaps has any of us suffered so much as this ugly, pitiable, truly tragic man. If at first he repels us, and he should, gradually we are drawn to feel with him, as Verdi shows in him something of the potential for evil and for good that lies within ourselves.

How can we explain the immense amount of feeling Verdi found for the fathers in his works? How explain the powerful ambivalences, the hatred and the love? Some will say, look to Verdi's own experience. There was constant tension, and eventually bitterness, between Verdi and his own father, who seems never to have understood him. Verdi always felt more affection for Antonio Barezzi, who welcomed him early into his household and eventually gave him his daughter in marriage. "He loved me like his own son," Verdi wrote of Barezzi, "and I loved him as my father."

Then Verdi became a father himself; Virginia Barezzi bore him a daughter and a son. Both of them died in childhood, followed shortly thereafter by their mother. Verdi took the succession of shocks stoically, even—like his jester—fulfilling his commission to write a comedy in the midst of his sorrow. Then when that comedy, understandably, failed, he wrote only tragedy for fifty years. And always he seems to have looked, consciously or unconsciously, for dramatic subjects that would allow him to express in music the paternal affection he could never give to children of his own.

But of course it is not enough merely to look to an artist's life to understand his art. Any Italian will tell you that Verdi sang as much for his country as for himself, and no composer ever loved his country more. Verdi's father figures, be they Spaniard or Frenchman, Babylonian or Ethiop, are always, beneath their makeup, Italian to their very souls. They are nineteenth-century Italian realizations of that figure from Italian prehistory, the paterfamilias with power of life and death over his children, the patriarch whose rights were codified four centuries before Christ in the *Twelve Tables*. Perhaps, then, we should say that Verdi's fathers are so powerful because he wrote in a centuries-old Italian tradition that reveres the father as no other European tradition does.

I feel that I know that tradition fairly well, not just from listening to Verdi for half a century, not just from seeing over and over the neorealist films that project Verdi's themes in their own medium, not just from living in Italy through one of the most memorable years of my life, but also from teaching and writing on and wondering about Virgil, the Latin poet who is central to the patriarchal tradition, who made the founding hero of his Italy *pater Aeneas,* a father who escaped from flaming Troy with his father on his back and his little son at his side—*pius Aeneas,* a hero dedicated by the virtue of *pietas* to faith, family, and country. Nineteen centuries later, Verdi's father Rigoletto acknowledges that threefold tradition. "Culto, famiglia, la patria," he sings to his daughter. "Faith, family, country—you are all of them to me." Virgil's father Aeneas saw the human condition as *lacrimae rerum,* "a world of tears," and twenty centuries later Verdi's fathers sing "Piangi, piangi" to their children as they face their sufferings.

In Italy it is the father who presides over the only permanent social unit: the family. Governments, occupying forces, kings, popes, political regimes come and go, but the family is always there, providing the pattern for the larger structures of state and even church. In Italy every priest is called Father, and the supreme priest is called Papa. Understanding this patriarchal tradition, so strong in Virgil and Verdi, is the beginning of understanding many things about Italy that confound the non-Italian, from papal infallibility to *The Godfather.* Italy's long patriarchal tradition is not without its dangers, as Verdi's operas tell us again and again. But no one really understands

Verdi, or Italy, who does not understand that tradition, for it shaped both country and composer.

And yet, when all that is said, we still haven't explained why people far beyond Italy, people all over the world, respond when Verdi's fathers sing. In one performance of *The Sicilian Vespers* Verdi made an Italian father, cast as a Frenchman and singing in German, speak directly to this Irish-American son. Verdi stirred feelings in me I had forgotten I had, and reminded me of the human condition I share with every other father's son. He read my heart. He said what I could never say. That kind of gift transcends the artist's personal experience, transcends even the tradition, however long and powerful, in which the artist creates. For that kind of gift—the understanding of the human heart—there is, ultimately, no explanation.

PATTERNS
OF LIGHT

Simon Boccanegra

Simon Boccanegra is almost invariably called a sombre work, a dark work. That is why light is so important an element in it.

Take the opening prologue. We are in Genoa, in the fourteenth century, in the square before the church of San Lorenzo. It is night. Paolo, perhaps the darkest of Verdi's villains, stands in the shadows and plays on the superstitions of the crowd: "Do you see that dark palace, the evil fortress of the Fieschi? There's a beautiful girl immured there . . . and often at night, through the empty rooms, a strange light goes wandering, like an unquiet soul."

Suddenly a light flashes within, and the listeners cross themselves in fear.

Soon we hear that the beautiful girl in the darkened house, Maria, has died. Her grieving father, Fiesco, steps from his palace and says that he will never enter it again. He looks up to a statue of the Virgin on his balcony. The only light is a votive candle flickering before it. He reproaches the Virgin

25

Mary, for she did not protect the virginity of his Mary, his daughter Maria.

A little later, in the darkness, the young buccaneer Boccanegra enters. For six years he has been unable to see his beloved Maria because Fiesco would never pardon him for getting her with child. Now, on an impulse, Boccanegra tries the palace door and, to his amazement, finds it open. Fiesco has purposely left it open. The older man stands in the darkness, waiting to be avenged on the young man, waiting to hear his cry of despair when he finds his Maria dead.

The palace is so dark that Boccanegra comes outside, onto the balcony, to get that votive candle. Then he passes back into the darkness. All we see is the gleam of that symbol of virginal purity as we hear Boccanegra's despairing cry from within.

So the story of Boccanegra, which name can mean "a tale of darkness," begins with symbolic light. And so too, it ends. By the final scene, Boccanegra has ruled his turbulent city for twenty-five years. A last revolution has been quelled. From the ducal palace we look out across the city, to the sea. It is night. The captain of arms stands on the balcony and addresses the citizens: "By order of the doge, let all lights of the city be extinguished in honor of the dead who fell bravely." A trumpet blows, and Boccanegra enters—the doge come to honor the dead. Actually, he is dying himself, for his former friend Paolo has poisoned him. It is a terrible, slow-working poison, and Boccanegra dies slowly, painfully, but like a great ruler—pardoning, winning pardon, reconciling. And all the while we watch, from the balcony, the lights of the city going out, one by one, till Boccanegra dies himself.

The action that passes between those two light-and-darkness scenes may seem confused because it has to condense a sprawling and eventful play traced from a sprawling and eventful time. But the opera is clear and consistent in its symbols, its characters, and its music. The unifying elemental symbol throughout is the sea. Not the infinite sea of *Tristan,* or the vindictive sea of *Idomeneo,* or the tormented sea of *Peter Grimes.* In *Simon Boccanegra* we hear, in light and darkness, the sea that is the very life of Boccanegra's maritime city, Genoa.

I've always thought of the opening measures of the opera's prologue—gentle and darkly comforting—as suggesting the night sea that embraces these somber historical events. And surely the music that opens the first act is a seascape. We look out across the expanse of the sea at the moment when the stars go out and the moon sinks and the dawn comes up. Early morning winds transform the sound of distant church bells, making them sound like Debussy's engulfed cathedral. As the light glints on the surface of the sea, the winds whistle across it. Through Verdi's evocative music, the sea becomes linked in our minds with the city it protects, and with the young girl—the daughter of the Maria who died in the lightless palace—who, after Verdi's maritime prelude, enters to sing her seascape aria.

Jules Massenet, the composer of *Manon* and *Werther,* once traveled through Genoa, passing, in his own words, "gleaming landscapes, sun and sparkling seas." Verdi was living in Genoa at the time, eighty years old, and Massenet thought, "Quick, where does Verdi live?" The two composers met, and talked about music for half an hour. And then, Massenet records, "Verdi drew me to the terrace, from where we looked out on the marvelous harbor of Genoa. I shall always see him, bare-headed and upright beneath the scorching sun, showing me the iridescent town and the golden sea beneath us, with a gesture as proud as his genius and as simple as his beautiful artist's soul. It was almost as if he were one of the great doges of the past, stretching over Genoa his powerful and beneficent hand."

Reading that, you have to think not just of Amelia's sky-and-sea aria but of a passage near the end of the opera, where the dying Boccanegra gathers strength to look out on the sea he once sailed and loved. "O the coolness, O the breezes from the sea . . . il mare, il mare." In this opera, at a midpoint in his career, Verdi has found a kind of peace. Suffering, he knows, is inevitable in life. But people who suffer can nonetheless do great things. They make themselves great by rising greatly to meet their sufferings. And nature, the sea, gives lives a continuity and a permanence.

Boccanegra is a role prized by baritones. At the Metropolitan, Lawrence Tibbett and Leonard Warren and Sherrill Milnes have thought it the crowning achievement of their careers. At La Scala, Tito Gobbi has written, "I cannot describe the joy, the respect, the sheer love with which I have tried to serve this great work." All of these Boccanegras have found the role difficult. Verdi himself cautioned, "It is a role as tiring as Rigoletto, and a thousand times more difficult. In *Forza,* the roles are already there . . . But in *Boccanegra* . . . the role has to be made."

Verdi sensed that there were more facets to this complex role than even he, with his sympathetic understanding of both human nature and the baritone voice, could, in the space of a single opera, express. For Boccanegra is by turns pirate and patriot, lover and father, young man and old, ruler both foolish and wise, mastered by his feelings and master of them. But, as Leonard Warren remarked, rightly, the character develops consistently, and young Boccanegra's mistakes give him greater compassion for the failings of others when he grows older. Sherrill Milnes has called Boccanegra the greatest human being in French or Italian opera—avoiding the comparisons, sometimes made, with Hans Sachs and Boris Godounov from the German and Russian traditions, roles of comparable stature that only the fearless would call greater.

But I find that I respond almost as much to the unvarying figure who, for twenty-five years, stands opposed to Boccanegra: old Fiesco. Verdi wanted for this role "a deep voice with something inexorable and inflexible in it. Prophetic and sepulchral. Give me a low F and a voice of steel." Fiesco comes from a family of maritime warriors and diplomats, a family that provided the church with two popes and seventy-two cardinals. Something of that pride is in this lion of a man, but also a great capacity for affection. That is why the rich-voiced Ezio Pinza was so unforgettable in the role. He could convey both the pride and the tenderness that lie at the heart of this inflexible patriarch.

Given those two mighty men in confrontation, it is hard to say which is the more moving moment in this opera about fathers: the moment when Boccanegra recognizes that Amelia is his daughter or the moment when Fiesco recognizes that that same Amelia is the daughter of his daughter. In each case the man's hard surface cracks. The first moment is wonderful; the second, I think, ineffable. Fiesco has sworn that he will never forgive Boccanegra till the child of his child is given back to him. When that child stands before him, and old Fiesco can finally forgive, and his hatred gives way at last, Boccanegra looks at him incredulously. "Tu piangi," he says. "You are weeping." "Yes," says old Fiesco, "I weep. I hear the voice of heaven in what you tell me." And, to the plangent half-step musical phrases that Verdi had already used in *Rigoletto* and *Il Trovatore* to indicate tears, the man who longed for forgiveness and the man who for so long refused to forgive fall into each other's arms.

Sometimes Verdi works very simply in this opera. Boccanegra finds his daughter after many years and exclaims, in a falling octave, "Figlia." Boccanegra dies and his daughter exclaims, in the same falling octave, the simplest of all musical intervals, "Padre." But sometimes the thematic development is remarkably subtle. Amelia's compassionate "pace" in the Council Chamber scene:

is an idea perverted in the mind of the evil Paolo. The theme is soon darkened:

and darkened:

Eventually the second, third, and fourth notes of the theme are distilled into the motif that signifies poison, and that three-note motif is inverted into this shuddery sequence when Boccanegra drinks of the cup Paolo has poisoned:

But for all the ingenious motific devices at work, the greatest moments of the opera are the moments when Verdi seems to be singing himself, voicing through the orchestra his own compassion for these suffering people:

Perhaps that passage and the other great compassionate utterances in this work are not only Verdi weeping for his characters but, as Tito Gobbi puts it, "the heart of Verdi mourning over the remembrance of his own past sorrow." For Verdi too, like Boccanegra, lost a young wife. Like Fiesco, he lost a daughter. The opera's events touched his own life.

But most of us who love Verdi feel, too, that he is weeping for *our* sorrows, our lives. So D'Annunzio, in a famous poem on the death of Verdi, says:

His humanity swept over us like the singing sea of heaven.
He found his song in the very breath of all who suffer.
He loved and wept for us all.

Pianse ed amò per tutti! You can hear the truth of that in this opera that sings of darkness and light, of the sea, of the wind that sweeps over and breathes across it, and of the love and tears of great-hearted people who, we think humbly when the opera is done, are not all that different from ourselves.

CHIAROSCURO

Un Ballo in Maschera

It is often said that Verdi wrote only two comic operas, his youthful *Un Giorno di Regno,* which was a failure, and his last opera, *Falstaff,* which is often called his masterpiece. Through the fifty years that separate those two comedies, most people say, there was only tragedy on Verdi's stage: the deaths of lovers, friends, kings, and patriots.

In recent years, however, we have seen more deeply into *Un Ballo in Maschera.* It is true that, in this opera, lovers must part, friendship is betrayed, a king is killed, and misguided patriotism brings near ruin to a brilliant society. But all of that is cast into relief, something like comic relief, because the lover, the friend, the king, the object of the misguided patriotism is a bright, mercurial figure who rises to meet challenges with pluck and resourcefulness. He is the kind of hero we are used to meeting in comedy.

King Gustav is the most multifaceted of all the Verdi tenor roles. His whole life is a kind of masked ball. He is quick with disguises, and assumes one in each of the opera's three acts.

He seems to think that there is no problem that cannot be solved merely by the proper application of wit, daring, and appropriate style. We have to admire him in that, but—this too makes him a character of some dimension, and a human being like any of the rest of us—he is right only up to a point.

He is certainly right in the first act. He refuses to listen to the closed-minded councillors who want an accused witch hauled into court. Instead he suggests that the court take themselves off to see *her* and, under disguises, discover at first hand whether the charges against her are true. His suggestion is completely in character. It is not frivolous, as might at first appear. Gustav knows that the matter is too serious not to be taken lightly. The best way to defeat prejudice is to deflate it. The music that ends the first scene of *Ballo* is the surest indication of how this young king can rise resourcefully, laughingly, to meet any situation:

Gustav soon decides that the "witch" is harmless. Even when she predicts his death, his response is to laugh. (An early Gustav, Alessandro Bonci, with Verdi's approval, interpolated chuckles into the musical line of the quintet, "E scherzo od è follia," that defines the character of this versatile young ruler.)

But Gustav, like some of our own politicians and leaders, finds it easier to control potentially dangerous political situations than to control his own strong amorous instincts. Though he knows it is not right, he lightheartedly and wrongheadedly seeks out the wife of his best friend and most loyal subject. He finds her alone at the very moment when *she* has found, in a place of death, the herb that will make her forget him. In the duet he sings with her there, perhaps the most challenging love duet in Italian opera, we see the king for the first time not in control of himself. The disguise he assumes to escape detection in that place of death, the second of his three disguises, brings disgrace and disillusionment to those he has wronged.

But we are not allowed utterly to condemn this man. Verdi knows too much about the human heart, and human frailty, to permit that. The Gustav who loves to take dangerous risks is also the Gustav who, in his first words in the opera, declares that power is nothing unless it dries the tears of the unfortunate, that glory is nothing unless it be honorable. In the last act Gustav *is* honorable and honest with himself. He puts duty before personal happiness, and gives up his Amelia. In the last-act aria "Ma se m'è forza perderti" Verdi shows new depths in the man before he assumes his third and last disguise, at his own masked ball. That disguise brings him death. And at that last moment, as the mask falls to the floor, we see deepest into Gustav's nature. He really does have greatness in him. He takes on himself all the blame for what has happened, and forgives those who have killed him.

This is a man who lives life generously and wittily, who lives daringly on the brink, and is brought down by his own lighthearted recklessness. He is a comic figure caught in tragedy. I think he really knows that tragedy awaits him, and yet for most of the opera the side of him we see is the elegant jester who flirts with danger. That is why he is companioned by a quicksilver page boy, himself a kind of persona or mask, who in scene after scene lets us see only his master's comic view of life.

Verdi was attracted by the chiaroscuro—the contrasts of light and darkness, of comic and tragic—in this subject. Actually, he was preparing, the year he wrote about this brilliant young king, to write a different opera, on another, older, grander king who also has a weakness that brings his kingdom to ruin: King Lear. Shakespeare's drama is another, and of course greater, study in chiaroscuro—a shocking, annihilating tragedy streaked with brilliant, caustic humor, from Lear's fool to the simulated madness of Poor Tom to the fool's madness of Lear himself.

Verdi did not write *Lear* because he and his librettist, Antonio Somma, were under commission to Naples, and in 1859 Naples couldn't provide the singers for something so vast as *Lear*. Verdi may also have felt, in midcareer, that he wasn't yet ready for the challenge of Shakespeare's old mythical king. So he turned to a younger historical king, to Gustavus III of Sweden, who really had been assassinated at a masked ball in Stockholm some sixty-five years earlier. The story of the assassination had already been made into a play by Scribe and set to music by other composers. In fact, Auber's opera on the subject had been performed more than a hundred times at the Paris Opéra. But Verdi was sure he could do more than the others with the subject. And he did.

What had actually happened sixty-five years before in Stockholm? Here I'll take a leaf from Charles Osborne's informative book, *The Complete Operas of Verdi*. Gustavus III of Sweden was, like his contemporary Joseph II of Austria, a hard-line liberal. He was also brave in battle, loved by his people, and skilled in the arts. He kept a court famous for its culture and scholarship, and he founded the Swedish Academy, which, since 1901, has awarded the Nobel prize for literature. He was ahead of his time with democratic ideas, but also autocratic in ways that, with the changing times, seemed almost calculated to turn some subjects against him. He knew that there were plots brewing, and occasionally he visited a local seer named Madame Arvedson, not because he thought her a genuine clairvoyant but because he knew she had a pipeline to court gossip.

The fatal conspiracy against him was hatched by the two noblemen we meet in the opera: Counts Ribbing and de Horn, whose privileges the king had abrogated. They won to their cause a disaffected and fanatical ex-army captain named Ankarström. And at the Royal Opera House Ball in 1792, Ankarström shot the king in the back with a pistol loaded with rusty nails, so that gangrene would do the work if nothing else did. The king lingered on in great pain for thirteen days, and in that time he pardoned the conspirators. All the same, when the king died, Ribbing and de Horn were exiled, and the unrepentent Ankarström had his shooting hand lopped off. Then his body, decapitated, was drawn and quartered and hanged in the public square.

It's a fascinating bit of history. But I sometimes wonder if Verdi would have set it to music if he had known all that lay in store for him. His opera almost went through the torments of the dying Ankarström. In 1857, the political censors were apprehensive about anyone's depicting an assassination on the stage—and with good cause. Italy was then divided into eleven states and kingdoms, occupied by Austria, convulsed by wars, conspiracies, and insurrections. In the Naples where *Ballo* was to be performed, King Ferdinand had, only a few months previously, barely escaped an assassination attempt. The very day Verdi arrived in Naples, three bombs were thrown by an Italian patriot in Paris at the carriage of Napoleon III and his wife, Eugénie. Eight people died in that incident, and 150 were injured. More than that, Verdi's librettist, Somma, was under police surveillance for his participation in uprisings against the Austrians in Venice, and he chose to write the *Ballo* libretto under a pseudonym. And Verdi himself had had problems with political censors for fifteen years. But the changes the censors had demanded in *Nabucco, Ernani, La Battaglia di Legnano,* and *Rigoletto* were nothing compared to what he had to face now.

It was suggested, and in some performances it came to pass, that the locale of *Ballo* be moved from Sweden to remote Pomerania or medieval Italy or even colonial Boston. That there be no death by firearms. That the king become a duke or a governor or even a private citizen. That Amelia (the only main character without a historical counterpart) become the king's sister. That, in the Boston version, the clairvoyant and the conspirators and the assassin all be made mulattos or blacks.

The Boston setting is in fact the version in which the opera became familiar, and many who know the opera well will call Gustav Riccardo, and Madam Arvedson Ulrica, and Ankarström Renato, and the conspirators Samuel and Tom. Those are the names in the text that Verdi finally set, and we still hear those stopgap names today in the arias and recitatives. In fact, as nineteenth-century history loomed over the history of *Un Ballo in Maschera,* more than a third of the original text had to be changed. When Verdi balked at this, the management of the San Carlo in Naples brought legal action against him for breach of contract. He was even threatened with arrest and imprisonment.

In the end, Verdi completed *Un Ballo in Maschera,* and the premiere finally took place in Rome, with the Boston setting. The opera survived. It was then and still is strong enough to weather whatever locale, northern or southern or transatlantic, a director chooses to set it in. Its music is on a par with that in *La Traviata* or *Il Trovatore*—though, subtly blended as it is of comic and tragic styles, it is less easily accessible than they. We are never quite at ease with it. Perhaps the only aria from *Ballo* immediately to establish itself and continue for more than a century as a popular favorite is that unambivalent aria for the baritone, written in Verdi's richest and clearest tragic vein, "Eri tu." No one would say that that unambiguously tragic piece is anything less than great operatic music. And yet no one has really risen to the test of *Un Ballo in Maschera* who has not followed its splendidly ambivalent main character, call him Gustav or Riccardo, through the series of tragic events lit with flashes of his own wit, daring, generosity, and—in the end—nobility. It is the curious symbiosis of comic and tragic in the character of its king that gives *Ballo* its very special quality.

When the opera is over, we wonder, "Was the seer in Act I right? Was it really fate that struck down the king?" In other Verdi operas, like *Il Trovatore* and *La Forza del Destino,* works that convey the composer's relentlessly pessimistic view of the world, it *is* a cruel and impersonal fate that destroys human lives. We *could* say the same about *Ballo,* that Ulrica (or Madam Arvedson) really saw from the start that it was fated that the king would soon be killed. But if instead we say, and I think we should, that it was the king's own contradictory character—his devil-may-care disregard for himself and his touching regard for others—that destroyed him, then we can see how special *Un Ballo en Maschera* is among the Verdi operas.

All of us who love Verdi regret that he didn't write his Shakespearian *King Lear* in 1857. Some Verdians have wishfully supposed that at some time he actually did write *Lear*: Franz Werfel's novel *Verdi* climaxes in a scene where a despairing Verdi, after a silent encounter with his rival Wagner in Venice, burns the completed score of *Lear*. Today, critics are content to say that ideas for Verdi's lifelong obsession with *King Lear* went into the father-daughter scenes in such pre-*Ballo* operas as *Giovanna d'Arco, Luisa Miller, Rigoletto,* and *Simon Boccanegra*. We know that some of Somma's libretto for *Lear* went into *La Forza del Destino,* and that, after *Otello* and *Falstaff,* when Verdi was eighty-three, Boito suggested *Lear* to him one last time.

Verdi never rose to the challenge of the old Shakespearian king. But he did write, in the face of tremendous odds and out of a piece of history that no other dramatist had seen very deeply into, a tragicomedy about a younger king, less archetypal than King Lear but nonetheless a figure to stand for any of us flawed human beings—a good man who fought to control his passions, who laughed because he knew there were some things too deep for tears, who loved life and lived it more wittily than well, who fell because of human frailty but, in the end, showed his love for his people, and perhaps saved his kingdom, in an act of sublime forgiveness.

A young king of splendid ambiguity. And an opera in which comedy and tragedy come together.

EVERYTHING
IN THIS DRAMA
IS TRUE

Don Carlo

I want to begin this discussion by citing some truly shocking words about *Don Carlo*:

> Everything in this drama is false. The real Don Carlo was a fool, a madman. Elisabeth was never in love with him. Rodrigo is a complete fiction; he could never have existed under King Philip. Philip wasn't as soft-hearted as that. In this drama there is nothing historical. Nor is there any Shakespearian truth, or profundity.

Who could have dared make such remarks about *Don Carlo*? Some German literary critic at the first performance of Schiller's original play? No, for though Schiller's character Rodrigo *was* criticized as unbelievable, and Schiller felt compelled to write a lengthy defense of him, the rest of the play conformed largely to what Schiller's sources and his German contemporaries knew of, or at least accepted as true about, sixteenth-century Spain.

Well then, are these the words of some French music critic, at the premiere of the opera Verdi based on Schiller? More likely. The Paris press was critical of the work their Opéra had commissioned from Verdi, and their century knew much more than Schiller's did about Philip II and his Spain.

But no—the intemperate phrases were written by Verdi himself. And he wrote them to Ricordi, his publisher. This was some seventeen years after the Paris premiere. Verdi was now preparing the work, in Italian, for La Scala. The opening act, set in France, would be cut, its tenor aria transferred to a later place. The opera would be set wholly in Spain, and would begin and end at the monastery of San Yuste. But, after seventeen years, Verdi still hadn't settled his artistic conscience on the matter of the monk at San Yuste, the figure who, at the opera's start, speaks mysteriously to young Carlo at the tomb of Charles V and, at the opera's end, issues from the tomb of Charles V to rescue Carlo from the Inquisition. There was no such rescue in Schiller, let alone in history.

Verdi's libretto suggests that the monk might actually be the ghost of Charles V, or even Charles V still alive, come to rescue his grandson. There is in fact a hint in history that Charles did not die when his subjects thought he did but lived on for years in monastic seclusion. But Verdi knew that the libretto for his opera left this unclear, that the deus-ex-machina ending had never convinced audiences, who were left wondering, "Is the apparition a monk of San Yuste, or the ghost of the former king, or that former king himself, still alive?"

In his seventieth year, Verdi wanted to settle the matter finally: let the ghostly figure, when it reappears at the end, be fully revealed as King Charles V, still alive, in full royal regalia. And if the rescue had never happened, well, because everything else in the drama was false, "one thing more or less wouldn't do any harm." Verdi's words.

Rueful and astonishing words, especially for those who, in recent years and in increasing numbers, have come to see *Don Carlo* as Verdi's masterpiece. But we ought not to be utterly astonished at the rue, or ready to take the words at face value. Verdi was an immensely complicated man, shrewd with his collaborators, systematically self-effacing, and sometimes (as in the well-known case of his calling the premiere of *La Traviata* a fiasco) inclined to see failure where success did not live up to his exacting standards.

The shocking words are mainly useful, then, for clearing the air before any discussion of the characters in *Don Carlo*. Neither Verdi nor Schiller was writing history. What Verdi and, before him, Schiller had written were great works of art.

The glory of Schiller's play is in its ideas: its dramatization of the tensions between liberalism and absolutism, its sense of the complexities and ambivalences of political action. The glory of Verdi's opera is in the characters—the five characters so untrue to history but so true to life, each of them influencing and influenced by the other four, all of them interdependent, all of them depicted in music of immense understanding and compassion. Verdi turned Schiller's drama of ideas into five interlocking tragedies. In the opera we see five characters, each equal in importance, each seen in prismatic relationships with the other four. It is even possible to say that each of them is, in some way, in love with the other four. But, in this opera of ambivalences, we find that there is hate commingled with that love.

Let's talk about the five characters one by one.

In many ways, the most moving of them is the one we have, at first, the least sympathy with: King Philip. Verdi once visited the king's room in the Escorial and was amazed, as most visitors are, at its austerity, at the "wretched little bed" on which the powerful man recruited his strength. He must also have noticed that the only other furniture in the room was the prie-dieu at which the same man prayed. Verdi's King Philip is an absolutist because he believes in the absolute rightness of his faith. Privately, though, he is vulnerable. He is dominated by the Grand Inquisitor who has made him and can easily unmake him. And he is unloved. His wife is unresponsive because of his suspicions of her, and his son hates him for his brutal use of force. So he must find consolation in a surrogate wife, Eboli, though she plays for power, and a surrogate son, Rodrigo, though that young man dares to challenge him on matters of church and state. King Philip tries to love them all, but from none of them does the love he tries to give come back to him. He could almost sing the aria about his wife, "She never loved me," to any one of the others.

Eboli is similarly loving and unloved. Her "don fatale"—that fatal gift, her beauty—is rejected by the others as much as ever is Philip's power. She draws gallant compliments from Rodrigo, but he knows better than to trust her. She has an adulterous relationship with the king, but he knows that he can never publicly acknowlege her. She plots against the prince and the queen, out of passion for the one and jealousy of the other, and though she comes in the end to respect and even love them both, nowhere is her aggressive affection returned. She is characterized at the very first by her "Veil Song"—where she sings how a Moorish king once invited a veiled beauty to share his throne because he was tired of his queen. In the song the beautiful woman lifts her veil and reveals herself *to be* the unloved queen.

The "Veil Song" in effect unveils its singer: Eboli does not realize its implications, how it shows that she is duplicitous, secretly ambitious, destined to fail. Twice in the action that follows we think back to the song. First, when Carlo approaches Eboli in the moonlight, thinking she is the queen, and then exclaims, as she removes her disguise, "It is *not* the queen!" And again, when the queen confronts Eboli over the stolen jewel case, and Eboli discovers that, all along, it was not she but the queen whom King Philip had really loved. The song was right. Eboli, traditionaly blind in one eye, is like the symbolically one-eyed figures in myth: she knows everything that happens around her, and nothing of herself. Her tragedy is not much different from that of Philip, of whom Rodrigo says, "You rule the world, and you cannot rule yourself."

Then there is the queen, Elisabeth. She falls in love, innocently enough, with the prince before she knows he is the prince—and then the news comes that for reasons of state she must marry not him but his father. Her innocent love then forever after appears to be guilty. But in her weakness, the queen is strong—stronger than both Eboli and King Philip when they falsely accuse her. She knows that they are guilty together not just of the adultery but of the hypocrisy they have charged her with. In her final aria, "Tu che le vanità," she sees into the essential loneliness each of the five characters shares, the vast sweep of history into eternity in which each of them is caught.

The title character, Don Carlo, is similarly affected by the other four. He cannot respond to his tyrannical father or the devious Eboli, however much they ask for his love. He gives his heart instead to the noble ideas of Rodrigo, seeing in them a way of sublimating the passion he is forbidden to express for the queen. She reminds him of the Oedipal nature of that passion ("Will you kill your father and then, stained with his blood, lead your mother to the altar?"), and indeed at the center of the opera Carlo does, like Oedipus, draw his sword against his father. Then, in the last-act duet, Elisabeth awakens him to a transcendent reality, and he has the greatness of soul to respond in it.

But perhaps the finest character in the opera is the last of the five, that less-than-historical creation of Schiller's, Rodrigo, the Marquis of Posa. For Schiller he is the embodiment, in the midst of sixteenth-century oppression, of the new eighteenth-century ideals of tolerance, political and religious freedom, and universal brotherhood. For Verdi he is all of that and, operatically speaking, something more. He is a baritone; Verdi never failed his baritones, nor they him.

Rodrigo is in the great tragic line of Verdi baritones, brave as the two cornets that adorn his soldierly death. In his exchanges with the other four characters, Rodrigo invariably says what must be said to keep the dangerous private situation under control, but he keeps in mind as well the concerns of a larger public world of war and peace. The other four all trust him. At first we wonder why, for his actions appear to be questionable. Why, when King Philip tells him he suspects that the queen and the prince are lovers, does Rodrigo agree to spy for him? Why does he threaten to kill Eboli? Why does he ask Carlo, who by then knows of his collaboration with the king, to hand over any incriminating documents? Why does he later force Carlo to surrender his sword and accept imprisonment, while he himself accepts political advancement? Why does he arrange for Carlo to meet the queen where the king will ultimately find the two of them together? In Schiller, there is a clear answer to most of these questions: the high-minded Rodrigo is a manipulator who will stop at nothing to realize his noble ideals. In Verdi, we cannot feel that way about him. All along, Verdi's Rodrigo takes responsibility and suspicion on himself. Always he is there in the thick of things, trying to do what has to be done. Some of the time he fails. But all of the time he does what he thinks is right. And the music says the rest.

So Verdi's opera moves from one ambivalent character, from one shifting situation, to another. This complexity may be one reason for *Don Carlo*'s taking so long to achieve its present critical and popular acceptance. (It was out of the repertory of the Paris Opéra, where it premiered, for almost a century, and when Rudolf Bing revived it at the old Met, it hadn't been done there for almost thirty years.) In no other Verdi opera, not even in the two final Shakespearian works, is there the prismatic shifting of characters in situations that we find in *Don Carlo*. This kind of drama, an ensemble drama in which no character is complete until seen in complex relationships with each of the others, is what Mozart put on the operatic stage—and significantly, Mozart's operas too have come to full acceptance only in recent decades.

Don Carlo may not be true to history. But it is true to the way the finest dramatists have made history into drama. It is true, psychologically and powerfully true, to life—to life's ambivalences and uncertainties and ironies. It is true in its near despair over human attempts at self-understanding. What it says about self-understanding was once summed up memorably by John Freeman in *Opera News*: "We hardly know ourselves. . . . [W]e know ourselves less when with others, and know others even less than that. The message is pessimistic, and Verdi was an eloquent pessimist."

Not, however, a complete pessimist. At the midpoint in *Don Carlo,* Verdi uses his orchestra to answer the hatred of history's oppressors with consolation for history's oppressed:

That orchestral voice—Verdi's own personal comment—is later affirmed by a voice from heaven singing the same melody. Most modern productions are embarrassed by this. Jean-Pierre Ponnelle, in a Hamburg production, showed on stage a reform movement trumping up the heavenly voice as a kind of counterdemonstration. So doth our presumed sophistication make cowards of us all. Verdi wanted the affirmation of that pronouncement from heaven. He wanted to attest to the existence of a loving, providential power above and beyond the dynamics of history and the uncertainties of human relationships.

That, I think, is why he kept his apparition from the tomb, his King Charles still alive, at the end. He knew it was a crude device, unsatisfactory, unhistorical, and unlikely to convince the sophisticates. But he knew as well that it said what Schiller had not said. It saves Don Carlo so that Rodrigo's death is not in vain. It effects what Eboli, in her plan to rescue Carlo, could not do. It leaves the king struck with awe at a power beyond his own. And it prompts the queen to sing, as the last radiant—and, I like to think, affirmative—syllable in the opera, "Ciel!" ("Heaven!").

Nothing in the ending is spelled out for us. Verdi didn't try to explain it, even to his publisher. We can make of it what we will. We can even think it false if we dare to. I for one am prompted to turn Verdi's words around and say that, as a reading not of history but of the human heart, "Everything in this drama is true." And I have the feeling that the profound and perceptive composer of *Don Carlo* would be stern with me for contradicting him, and then would tell me, not that I am right, but that I have the right to think as I do.

SIX
PROPHETIC
TRUMPETS

Aida

The first time you hear *Aida,* there is one moment you wait
for with growing excitement because you've heard about it all
your life. In fact, I remember being quite sick with excitement
when, at the age of twelve, I was taken by my mother to my
first *Aida* and, a few minutes into the triumphal scene, I heard
a choir of trumpeters play the tune I'd heard about all my life:

It's hard to say what makes the march from *Aida* so remarkable. There are only five notes in it, and a sixth for decoration.
Just the notes a bugler sounds when playing taps, and two
passing notes that might, with the others, have once been
sounded on the long, straight, valveless instrument that was
the only trumpet known to antiquity.

Archaeology was an exciting new science when *Aida* was written. Heinrich Schliemann unearthed Homer's Troy the very year of *Aida*'s premiere, and other excavations were revealing much of ancient Egypt itself. Verdi wanted archaeological correctness in his Egyptian opera. Specifically, he wanted that ancient trumpet on stage, and he had six of them specially made in Milan. Then he found, to his disappointment, that they needed a small valve if modern musicians were going to play his march tune on them.

Even with the valves neatly hidden under the players' hands, the march was something of a gamble. Restricting himself to just six brassy notes for the great moment at the center of his opera might have resulted in a sound not grandly barbaric but embarrassingly primitive.

Well, Verdi had a way around that. After three of his long trumpets have played the tune in the key of A-flat, he has the other three, pitched three semitones higher, repeat it from across the stage in their new register. So the march gets an exciting lift halfway through, as the second choir of trumpets takes over in the higher key of B-natural. Then Verdi restores the march to its earlier key, A-flat. And there he contrives, in a simple but very telling effect, to have the two sets of trumpets play together, using as a descant the only note the second set has in common with the first:

That's a device that even a twelve-year-old boy can appreciate. Yet it works as effectively on the stage as anything Meyerbeer or Berlioz had devised with more sumptuous means. It sounds grandly barbaric. And, without knowing it, Verdi *was* archaeologically right about the trumpets. When King Tut's tomb was opened in 1925, two trumpets were found within, one tuned in A-flat, the other in B—incredibly, the very two keys Verdi had used.

Verdi had to be persuaded to write the opera that contains that famous march. He was as old then as I am now: not quite an old man, but almost. He had written twenty-three operas, and he wanted to retire to his farm. The old battles were won. The unification of Italy, from any ideological point of view the main subject of his early work, had been accomplished. He had every reason to feel that he had done his life's work, and done it very well. But surely part of the reason for his retirement was that he felt the musical world gravitating toward the German operatic titan, Richard Wagner. And Verdi's taste and temperament were not Wagner's.

All the while, one of his Paris librettists, Camille du Locle, who was sure that Verdi still had a lot of music in him, kept trying to interest him in further projects. And one day the post brought Verdi a suggestion from du Locle that caught his attention. It was a four-page synopsis for an opera for Cairo, to be set in ancient Egypt. It was a simple story—the conflict of love and duty—with clearly etched characters and the kind of strong situations Verdi knew music could dramatize. "Ma chi l'ha fatto?" he asked. "But who wrote it?"

Du Locle played a mild deception. He gave the impression that the story had been written in part by the khedive of Egypt himself—the munificent Ismail Pasha, the first of the three viceroys appointed by the Ottoman Empire to rule Egypt before World War I, during the building of the Suez Canal.

I don't think Verdi ever fully believed that the story was the khedive's. But he did know, and said as much, that "behind it was the hand of an expert."

Du Locle probably got the synopsis from an old acquaintance newly come to fame, Auguste Mariette. A lowly cataloguer at the Louvre, Mariette had been dispatched by the

French government to Cairo to acquire some Coptic manuscripts and, finding the monastery doors closed to him, had spent the money, without authorization, on archaeology. He was lucky in the Egyptian sands; he discovered the first of the hundred sphinxes guarding the approach to the serapeum at Sakkarah, and after that he was responsible for several of the most important Egyptian finds of the nineteenth century, including the temples and tombs at Giza, Abydos, Karnak, and Thebes. He was given the title of bey and made inspector general of monuments by the khedive. And now the lucky Mariette had a story that, put to music, was to sweep the world: *Aida*.

There has always been some doubt as to whether the story really was Mariette's. But he had the beginnings of it in his own experience; he'd actually uncovered a walled-up skeleton when excavating his serapeum. And he had a decided flair for the theatrical. He used to take tourists through his serapeum with underground light provided by two hundred boy torchbearers positioned in the niches between the great sarcophagi, with the stillness punctuated by popping magnesium flares and blazing Bengal lights.

Author of the story or not, Mariette was determined to get Verdi to set it to music, even though Verdi had already turned down two earlier offers to write something for Cairo. Mariette wrote to du Locle, slyly: "If M. Verdi does not accept, His Highness instructs you to knock at another door. Gounod and Wagner are being considered. The latter, if he is willing, could do something *really* grand."

That did it. Verdi's interest picked up instantly. He first sounded out the khedive by asking for an outrageous sum of money—150,000 francs, one of the largest commission fees of all time. The khedive came through with his promise in three days. So Verdi went to his piano again. And while Mariette traveled to Paris to design and execute the scenery in accordance with his professional specifications, du Locle left Paris to consult with Verdi on his Italian farm. In less than a week the four-page outline became, between the two of them, the four acts of *Aida,* in French prose.

Verdi then had the French translated into Italian verse by the man who had already helped him with the revisions of *La Forza del Destino* and *Don Carlo.* I think I would have trembled in my boots if ever I had come face-to-face with Verdi, but I would have loved sometime to have had a long talk with that other Italian who had a hand in the making of *Aida,* Antonio Ghislanzoni. He was a onetime seminarian, a medical student, a revolutionary; a double-bass player, a baritone, an impresario; a journalist, novelist, editor, critic—and often many of these at the same time. Something of a bohemian perhaps, but a bohemian who took Verdi's criticism humbly. And criticism there was. We have thirty-four of the letters that passed between the composer and the librettist, so we can still read how Verdi bullied Ghislanzoni till he got, instead of libretto language, the simple, heartfelt dialogue he wanted. Sometimes Verdi, tired of waiting, composed the music before he got Ghislanzoni's verses in the mail. He wrote his own Italian lines and set those.

So why not say what should be said? Verdi is the librettist of *Aida.* He insisted, in his arrangements with the khedive, that he have complete authority over the project. He collaborated with du Locle, and got what he wanted out of Ghislanzoni. He suggested some of the best details in the staging, including the split levels in the last act. In fact, the only thing in *Aida* he was not directly involved with was the first idea, the four-page outline. But what he said of those four anonymous pages we can say of the finished work: "Behind it is the hand of an expert." The hand of Verdi.

The music came quickly from the master's hand, music of a new richness and complexity, yet accessible even when heard for the first time. At the close of Act II, to end the Triumphal Scene, Verdi reprises the chorus that began it, "Glory to Egypt":

Then Ramfis and his priests sing their thanks to Egypt's gods:

Then Aida and Radames sing that all their happiness is ended:

For a moment, Aida's father sidles up to her, and whispers that his Ethiops will have revenge, and the music changes its tone. Then Verdi, in a burst of glory, combines all three of the previous melodies. It is a splendid moment, and I remember marking it, though I then had no special ear for complexity, when as a boy of twelve I first heard the Triumphal Scene.

Act III, the Nile Scene, has subtleties that astonish after a hundred listenings. It is among other things a master textbook on how to write evocatively for woodwinds. Under those winds it is as if we were sailing down the Nile by moonlight, past the pyramids, to a temple under swaying palm trees. Then, through the arias and duets that follow, flute and oboe, clarinet and bassoon wave and undulate in intricate patterns and conjure up the steamy, shimmering night, the ebb and swell of the river that rises in Aida's land and ends in the land of Radames. We hear that river's ooze and slime, its serpents, fishes, insects, birds, and crocodiles. And almost all of this is in the woodwinds.

The vocal music in the Nile Scene is remarkable too—as impassioned and beautifully wrought as anything in Verdi. But wonderful as it is, it is surpassed by the duet "O terra, addio" in the last act. At first Aida and Radames sing separately. Then they blend their voices in soaring unison, voicing their farewell to earth in a great, spreading arc of melody while the whole orchestra seems to quiver in one vast, cosmic tremolo. In no other music is there anything to equal this feeling of leaving earth for sky, of quietly walking through space. This grandest of operas ends, as it begins, with music that is quiet, luminous, delicately nuanced.

The Cairo premiere of *Aida* was delayed for almost a year when the Franco-Prussian War broke out and Mariette and all the scenery were closed off in beleaguered Paris. Verdi set aside a large part of his advance payment to help the French wounded. He also said he wouldn't make the trip to Cairo, and he didn't. He did go to Milan for the Italian premiere six months later, and wrote for that some new music, including Aida's "O patria mia" in Act III. Both premieres were triumphs. And since then *Aida* has become perhaps the most popular opera in the world. For most of my lifetime it has been the most often performed opera at the Metropolitan, and the most often featured on the Saturday broadcasts.

But a great operatic success doesn't always mean triumph and fulfillment for its creators. For the creators of *Aida,* it was almost as if they'd inherited the curse laid on those who opened King Tut's tomb.

The khedive was dismissed by the Ottomans eight years after the *Aida* opening. His administrative policies, not all of them enlightened, eventually ran Egypt's national debt from seven million to an enormous one hundred million pounds. He ended his days back in Istanbul.

Mariette, within a few years, was advanced from Mariette Bey to Mariette Pasha, and commanded thousands of workmen at thirty-five archaeological sites. But meanwhile, cholera had claimed five of his children and, finally, his wife. Soon, declining health and dwindling resources had him borrowing money to pay his bills. Then the Nile flooded his house and most of his papers were ruined, and in a fit of despair he threw the rest of them into the river. But his fame survived him, and a bronze statue of him still stands on his sarcophagus in the main square in Cairo.

Du Locle took over the management of the Opéra-Comique in Paris, only to see it go bankrupt with the initial failure of Bizet's *Carmen*. He and Verdi had a falling-out, and almost went to court, over money the composer had advanced him. Reconciliation came years later, but du Locle ended up a disillusioned man, for all that he had had a hand in two of the most popular operas ever written.

And Verdi? He was angered that his new work, while widely admired, reminded some critics of Wagner. "If only I had never written *Aida*!" he said, ruefully. "To end up, after more than thirty-five years in the theater, an imitator!" We, with hindsight, have come to see *Aida* as not Wagnerian at all but as crafted dramatically along the lines of French grand opera and musically the vindication and renewal of Italian vocal art in the face of the onslaughts of German symphonic drama. But Verdi was so saddened about being praised for the wrong reasons that he went into another period of virtual retirement from opera. When he resurfaced sixteen years later, in his late seventies, after Wagner's death, it was to write the two greatest of all Italian works for the musical stage, the ultimate reconciliation in opera of the vocal and the orchestral—*Otello* and *Falstaff.*

Verdi was still alive when, in 1896, Italy invaded Ethiopia. He was furious. He had always sympathized with the downtrodden, and he detested colonialism. (*Aida* is certainly witness to that.) He did not think that such aggressive policies were what he and others had struggled their lifetimes for. "We are in the wrong," he said, "and we will pay for it." He was right. The sons of Amonasro gave the invading armies one of the worst defeats ever visited on a European power in colonial warfare. When Mussolini's reprisals came a generation later, Verdi was gone, but *Aida* still spoke for him.

Finally, Ghislanzoni. He never had another success like *Aida.* Though he wrote over eighty other librettos and published more than two thousand articles on all manner of subjects, his proudest moment remains, characteristically, his humblest. When Verdi received twenty-two curtain calls at the Milan premiere of *Aida,* he went backstage to look for Ghislanzoni, to give him his share of the applause. But his collaborator had left the theater. Always a witty man, and a wise one, Ghislanzoni knew that Verdi was, more than any of them, the creator of *Aida,* and the only one really to deserve credit for that triumphal scene, with those six prophetic trumpets.

THE HEART
OF DARKNESS

Otello

The first chord of Verdi's *Otello* flashes like lightning through the theater. It is a savage and destructive sound, elemental and full of fury. It is also, as our leading Verdian, Julian Budden, points out, as unresolved, as impossible to analyze harmonically, as that other chord—the one that changed the course of music for the past hundred years, the opening chord in Wagner's *Tristan*.

Sooner or later, in a discussion of Verdi, one must come to Wagner. Born the same year, 1813, the two masters from two different cultures on two different sides of the Alps dominate the whole of nineteenth-century opera, and to a large extent the whole of opera today. Certainly the two works that have most influenced the operatic output of our century are Verdi's *Otello* and Wagner's *Tristan*. And in both works, the initial chord, an evocation of the sea, is a way of understanding the opera to follow.

Tristan's first dissonant, unresolved chord expresses the human longing for the infinite that finds fulfillment only in death. It is a wonderful chord, and once it is struck there is nothing to do but to follow it onward, wave on wave, for hours till eventually it finds resolution.

Otello's initial chord is tougher, more frightening. It defiantly asks a question, perhaps the greatest question humankind has ever asked, and it leaves that question hanging in the air, over the stormy sea, unanswered. For Verdi there is no answer for it. His *Otello* asks, "What is God?" And Verdi was an agnostic.

Agnostics wonder. *Otello*'s unresolved initial chord makes us wonder about the power acting in the storm. The chorus sings that some terrible, blind, whirling spirit is ripping the heavens apart as if they were a veil. That word, "velo," is also the word Iago will use for the fatal handkerchief around which the plot revolves. "Velo" is Desdemona's word for the winding sheet that will receive her body. And its cognate, "una vela," a sail, the first words of the opera, marks the first sight of Otello's ship through the storm.

Those three lives—Iago's, Desdemona's, and Otello's—are ripped apart by the mighty force acting in the unresolved chord. We are almost compelled to see that force as malevolent. But the chorus are not so sure. Praying as the waves threaten Otello's fleet, they call the God they worship both "the lightning in the storm" and "the smile upon the shore." Later Otello and Iago, calling on their God to right their wrongs, swear by the lightning that is forked and the sea that exterminates. Is the force that spins the world a force of evil or of good? After a lifetime pondering the human condition, Verdi proclaims in *Otello* that we cannot know.

Nineteenth-century romanticism rediscovered Shakespeare, and no nineteenth-century composer knew Shakespeare better than Verdi, but Verdi's *Otello* is not Shakespeare's *Othello*. Every year hundreds of undergraduate essays cross English professors' desks, zeroing in on Iago, scrutinizing the arguments of Coleridge and Swinburne, Hazlitt and Lytton Strachey and Bernard Shaw, pondering why Shakespeare's Iago acts as he does. What are his motives? Can the whole mighty drama hinge on that despicable little passion we call jealousy?

Jealousy is important in the play. And it is certainly important in the opera, where Iago whispers to Otello, "Fear jealousy, my Lord. It is a dark, livid, blind monster that rips open a wound in its own breast and poisons itself." The image is powerful, and the music that expresses it sinister, but Shakespeare was concerned with more than jealousy, and Verdi knew it. A much mightier power is at work, and jealousy is only a monster it spawns. The famous Shakespearian A. C. Bradley once complained that *Othello* was the only one of the great tragedies that didn't suggest "huge universal powers working in the world." I don't think that that is really true of *Othello* and I know that it is not true of *Otello*. Verdi's opera plunges with its first chord into the heart of darkness. It is about God as well as man.

Because music requires more time than the spoken word to express itself, Verdi's librettist, Arrigo Boito, reduced Shakespeare's play by more than half. Surprisingly, then, he—or he and Verdi, for the two actively cooperated—felt that some things had to be added. Most of the additions are features a nineteenth-century Italian audience would expect, such as the bonfire chorus in Act I and the children's chorus in Act II. But two of the additions are large-scale extended solos, and they give the opera a dimension that the play, with the censorship imposed on the Jacobean theater, could not express. It is a religious dimension.

The first of the additions is Iago's "Credo." Some critics, like Paul Dukas, have thought it pretentious and childish. For others it is simply a matter of dramatic economy, compressing into one soliloquy a half dozen scenes from the play that the opera couldn't accommodate. But it is more than that. Traditionally the Credo is a declaration of the Christian faith. It has been part of the Catholic Mass for centuries. Medieval settings of it are still used, like this one that lifts upward as it says, "I believe in one God":

Cre-do in un-um De-um

Verdi's Iago begins with the same words, "I believe in one God," but he adds immediately, "A cruel god, who made me in his own image. And I call on him in hate." As a preface to this, Verdi's orchestra thunders out a savage parody of the old plain chant:

The Christian creed goes on to speak of human flesh as ennobled when God became incarnate, of human flesh as destined to rise from the grave. Verdi's Iago sings of the flesh as born from some vile element, a primeval slime he still feels within himself, destined only to corrupt in the grave, eaten by worms. The Christian creed speaks of man as capable of good. Verdi's Iago declares, "I am evil because I am a man." The Christian creed promises "the life of the world to come." Verdi's Iago sings, "This ridiculous life of ours ends in death, and then we are annihilated." After death, there is nothing: "Heaven is a folly passed on through the ages." There is nothing to believe in but an all-powerful, evil, cruel god.

With Verdi, the old problem in the undergraduate essay becomes irrelevant. His Iago says, "I believe with all my heart that the evil I think and the evil I do are really done through me by a higher power . . . I believe that man is the plaything of that power all his life." That is a far cry from Shakespeare's Iago, who initiates all his own schemes, and delights in the free exercise of his powers. Verdi's says, "I am driven on by a god from which there is no escape." And again, "Help me, Satan. Help my purpose." This Iago really is without a motive. He is possessed by evil, and that, in Verdi's new scheme, is motivation enough.

The opera's other large-scale addition to Shakespeare is also a liturgical piece, Desdemona's last-act "Ave Maria." At first sight it seems a completely unnecessary addition. Desdemona has already sung a full-length aria in the last act, a piece full of foreboding and pathos, the Shakespearian "Willow Song." Is a second aria, immediately following, really necessary? Verdi clearly thought so. He gives Desdemona an "Ave Maria" that is an extension of the traditional prayer, with extra details about heaven helping the oppressed, the humble, the innocent, to set against the hateful ranting in Iago's "Credo." The new "Ave Maria," like the new "Credo," is a character sketch of the one who sings it.

Verdi's heroine, undergraduates note with some surprise, is called, not Desdemóna, as in Shakespeare's English, but, after the Italian in Shakespeare's sources, Desdémona. The accent emphasizes the meaning of the two Greek words that form the name—*dys* and *daimon,* "evil" and "spirit." A strange name for this gentle, loving, trusting woman? Otello in his anger does not think so. He sees a demon in her hand in Act II, and actually calls her "demonio" in Act III. Then, in Act IV, when he has killed her and discovers too late that she is innocent, he explains the name: Desdémona is a "pia creatura nata sotto maligna stella." ("A trusting creature born under an evil star.") The name speaks the reality so painfully that Otello instantly exclaims, with emphasis on the accent, "Desdémona, Desdémona!"

Between Iago possessed by evil and Desdemona singled out by evil for destruction stands the unquestioned central figure of Verdi's opera, Otello himself. The composer eventually resisted his librettist's desire to name the opera *Iago*. He knew that the center of the drama, the real stage on which "huge universal powers" find their battleground, was the pure soul within the great black warrior who comes exultant out of the storm. The opera had to be called *Otello*.

It is not remarked often enough that in his most famous operas, Verdi extends sympathy to society's outcasts. The protagonist in *Rigoletto* is a hunchback, in *Il Trovatore* a gypsy, in *La Traviata* a prostitute, in *Aida* a black slave. Otello too is black. You often read that in Shakespeare's sources Otello was not black at all but a white Venetian with the surname Moro (Moor), and that in any case in the Renaissance the name would not imply so much "black" as "Islamic." But Otello is clearly black in Shakespeare's principal source, Cinthio's *Il Moro*. And in Shakespeare Othello is nothing less than the seventeenth-century image of the black man—a former slave, majestically innocent, a simple pagan who accepts an ambivalent Christianity. The color of his skin is important in Shakespeare, whose Venetians make abusive references to his "thick lips" and "sooty bosom." When Desdemona elopes with him, she is denounced in Venice as an abomination in the sight of God and men. People are sure that the Moor has used black arts to make her fall in love with him. But he defends himself nobly with lines Verdi was to use: "She loved me for the dangers I had passed / And I loved her that she did pity them." And she says, "I saw Othello's visage in his mind." It was "his honor and his valiant parts" that made her fall in love with him. His blackness is the drama's way of stressing his innocence and her courage. The color of his skin, which sets him apart, calls attention to the uniqueness of his heroic soul.

But he is vulnerable. As with Achilles' heel, as with the one spot on Siegfried's back, so there is with Shakespeare's Othello an outward manifestation of his vulnerability: his epilepsy. Verdi's Otello shows signs of it in each of the four acts, and he actually succumbs to an attack in the third. Otello the warrior can be destroyed. And, in the end, he is.

So, even more than the play, the opera, with its symbolic contrast of good in Desdemona and evil in Iago, and with Otello as the battlefield on which the forces play, comes close to the old mystery and morality plays out of which Europe's drama developed.

What was there in Verdi that responded to this symbolic Shakespearian libretto fitted out with two liturgical additions, one blasphemous and one devout? I feel that in the ambivalences, the extremes of evil and good, Verdi saw manifest his own problem with God. Whether God was a force of evil or of good he could not say. He knew only that innocent man must suffer, and stumble, and fall, and die.

As early as *Il Trovatore,* Verdi remarked, like his Iago, "Death is all there is to life. What else is there?" In the first version of *La Forza del Destino* he had the hero, a priest and a penitent, finally leap to his death in despair, shouting, like Iago, "I am the spirit of destruction. Let mankind perish. Extermination! Annihilation!" In his later years his wife, Giuseppina, said that Verdi was "happier believing nothing." When she asked him about God, he laughed in her face and said, though he loved her, "You are mad." "Life," he said near the end, "is such a stupid thing. What is worse, a pitiable thing. What do we accomplish? When all is said, there is only one humiliating answer—nothing."

On the other hand, though all his life he hated the triumphalism and temporal power of the church, and subscribed to no dogma, Verdi was, in Boito's words, "an example of Christian faith, in the moving beauty of his religious compositions and in his observance of rituals." Boito himself was an atheist, but he wrote of Verdi, "You must recall his noble head bowed in the chapel at Sant' Agatha. He knew that faith is the sustenance of the heart."

Verdi decided, eventually, to change the anarchic, atheistic ending of *Forza* for a scene of Christian forgiveness, possibly as a result of his meeting with old Alessandro Manzoni, whom he thought a saint. "If mortal men could be adored," Verdi said, "I would have knelt before him." It was at Manzoni's death that Verdi wrote his great Requiem Mass. As for his own funeral, he asked only that he be buried "modestly, either at dawn or at the evening *Ave Maria,* without any music."

All his life, Verdi valued his privacy. So, while we know much about his artistic convictions, we know only a little of the inner beliefs of the man himself. In the memorable phrase of Isaiah Berlin, Verdi was "a man who dissolved everything in his art." That art, a superb manifestation of the human spirit, does not give easy answers.

I have the feeling that Verdi's *Otello* means to leave its first defiant question forever unanswered. For me, *Otello* is an agnostic's statement: What God is, terrible or beautiful, we can never know in this life. The Manzoni Requiem I see as a similar statement. Just as *Otello* has both Iago's "Credo" and Desdemona's "Ave Maria," the Requiem has both the terrifying *Dies Irae* and the trusting *Lux Aeterna*.

But neither of these is Verdi's last word on God, man, and the meaning of life. The last word—that is to say, the last music—on those subjects is still another Latin liturgical piece: the *Te Deum* of the *Quattro Pezzi Sacri*. The devotional *Stabat Mater* may be even later, but it does not ask cosmic questions. The *Te Deum* does. It was the score Verdi wanted to take with him to the grave. It begins, again, with an old plainchant, reverently intoned, and it ends with the words, fifteen centuries old, "In Thee, O Lord, have I hoped. Let me never be confounded." The only solo voice in the work prays those words. The voice is answered by a single note on a trumpet coming nearer and nearer. Then the whole chorus supports the solo voice, singing "In Thee, O Lord, have I hoped." Finally there is a brief, graphic musical picture of a man dying. It is music very close to the music for the death of Otello—in the same key, with some of the same chord progressions. And it is, I need hardly say, very moving.

Each listener must decide for himself whether the end of Verdi's *Te Deum* says, "Death is all there is to life." Whether in the end it was Iago or Desdemona who claimed the old warrior's soul.

Parsifal
Courtesy Winnie Klotz, Photographer
Metropolitan Opera Association Inc.

THE
PHANTOM LOVER
AND THE
ETERNAL
FEMININE

Der Fliegende Holländer

Wagner first saw the fjords of Norway looming out of a storm. In his autobiography, *Mein Leben*—and let's say right off that that's a volume that needs to be taken with a grain of Saxon salt—Wagner tells us how he and his wife, Minna, and his big Newfoundland dog, Robber, fled angry creditors in Riga overland to northern Germany, and then proceeded over sea on a merchant ship bound for London, till a storm blew them off course and they put in for shelter at Sandwike, in Norway. Wagner remembered how "enormous granite cliffs echoed with the shouts of the men casting anchor and furling the sails."

It was from those sailors, he tells us, that he heard the story of the Flying Dutchman—how a defiant skipper once shouted into the blast that he would round the Cape of Good Hope even if he had to sail the sea till Judgment Day, how Satan heard him, wrote the compact in thunder and sulfur, and kept him from rounding the cape, kept him in fact forever on the sea, longing to die, awaiting judgment, suspended between heaven and hell.

That certainly sounds like an old sailor's yarn, but in fact in Wagner's day it was relatively new. Something of it may have derived from accounts of Vasco da Gama rounding the cape centuries before, and of course there were elements in it of Faust, selling his soul to the devil, and of Coleridge's Ancient Mariner, condemned to life-in-death on a phantom ship. But the Flying Dutchman himself appeared in print only a few years before Wagner took that perilous sea voyage. The Dutchman seems suddenly to have emerged, along with Dracula and the Frankenstein monster, in the nineteenth century, as if to prove that new myths could still surface in an industrial age.

The three nineteenth-century monsters have something gothically romantic in common. They are all frightening figures relentlessly striving for a redemption that always eludes them. The Flying Dutchman is a sailor's image of a damned soul, doomed to sail the sea till the day all humankind ascends to judgment, never to rest, never to die, till he passes into the void and is annihilated. (In the Metropolitan production he is captain on a voyage of the damned, bound forever in a seascape of snow and ice.)

The Dutchman was a figure that would have haunted the composer even if he had learned of it in less dramatic circumstances. The young Wagner was a romantic in the Gothic sense. As a boy he used to wake up screaming, imagining that objects in his room were alive. As a young man he loved Weber's *Der Freischütz,* with its wood-devil, and Marschner's *Der Vampyr,* with its Dracula story. As a fledgling conductor he knew those scores well. He also knew what it was to be lonely, rejected, and in flight. After that harboring in Norway in 1837 he was soon at sea again, passing through still more violent storms to London, and then across the Channel to Paris. There, he tells us, he endured humiliation and poor health and separation from his Minna when, for a time, he was confined to debtor's prison.

Meanwhile, he had found in a story by Heinrich Heine—a skeptical and cynical story he was to make archetypal and true—the suggestion he needed to complete the Dutchman's tale. Suppose that the haunted skipper is allowed ashore every seven years to search for a woman to redeem him with faithful love, and suppose that on one of those shores he should find a girl who throws herself into the sea to redeem him.

Wagner took the suggestion in Heine and shaped it into the first of his ten myths in music, with the first of his Liebestod endings, and the first of the lonely heroes who came to be figures for himself. Eventually he sent his Dutchman, with black-masted ship and blood-red sails, not to the Scotland of Heine's tale but to Norway, into the same Norwegian fjord he himself had seen. Wagner tells us he drafted his scenario in a single week, sold it in desperation to the Paris Opéra (and saw it handed over to a third-rate house conductor for composing), and finally, on a piano rented with his five hundred francs' payment, wrote in seven quick weeks his own music for the legend.

And with this new opera, after three previous works for the stage—works that showed talent but hardly genius—Wagner found himself at last as a composer of operas. The cumulative experience of flight, danger, loneliness, humiliation, and unrewarded striving for recognition—and the projection of these onto the figure of the Dutchman—all of these released in him creative forces of such power that he himself wondered in retrospect. He seemed of a sudden to have acquired an uncanny ability instantly to evoke and sustain an atmosphere, to have found a kind of sixth sense in setting nature to music. In *Der Fliegende Holländer (The Flying Dutchman)* the wild sea all but floods and fills the score. As one conductor said, "Open the score and a storm blows out at you on the instant."

Later, Wagner admitted that much of the youthful work was "imperfectly fashioned." He wanted an Erik "sombre as a northern headland" and a Daland "who defies storms and dangers." But the music he wrote for those subsidiary characters is often unhelpfully conventional. On the other hand, the orchestral writing is amazingly confident, the choruses are the most full-throated anyone in 1843 is likely to have heard, and, above all, the soliloquies and duets of Senta and the Dutchman are taut with the most single-minded intensity.

There more than anywhere lies the strength of the work. In his two main characters the intuitive Wagner for the first time touches on myth, which was to be the imaginative source of all his subsequent work. Wagner in fact brings two quite separate mythic figures face-to-face in this young man's opera, and finds that they were, all along, meant to meet. He presents, in Senta, the "eternal feminine." And, in the Dutchman, the "mysterious lover."

The "eternal feminine," (das Ewig-Weibliche) is one of the great themes of German romanticism, immortalized by Goethe on the last page of *Faust,* and familiar too on operatic stages in the works of Weber, Marschner, Meyerbeer, and especially in Beethoven's *Fidelio.* The "eternal feminine" is the ideal woman who releases a man from the prison of his self by understanding him and accepting and returning his love. At the time he composed *The Flying Dutchman,* Wagner described her romantically as "the redeeming woman who hovered before my vision . . . the quintessence of woman, longed for but beyond my dreams, ineffably womanly." The theme he gives Senta is accordingly consoling but elusive, leading onward and upward:

The "eternal feminine," in Goethe's words, leads a man upward. She has the power to lead him out of himself, not just because she is physically desirable but because she seems, from her intuitive understanding and acceptance of him, to be in touch with the sources of his being, the sources of his creative energies, the sources of wisdom itself.

I think it can be said that an "eternal feminine" appears in all of Wagner's subsequent work. Elisabeth, and Elisabeth alone, understands Tannhäuser and, like a star, leads him upward. Brünnhilde, on her mountain top, tells Siegfried that she has always known him, that she is his self. Isolde draws the delirious Tristan from the depths of his unconscious, and appears in a vision coming across the sea, walking on waves of flowers. Eva, seen in dreams as Eve, the Muse, and the Virgin Mary, draws stanza after stanza of inspired song from Walther. And the ambivalent Kundry gives Parsifal insight with a kiss. Only Elsa, in *Lohengrin,* seems at first not to fit the pattern—and yet it was Elsa of all Wagner's heroines who awakened him to a real understanding of this motif in his texts. "Elsa," he exclaimed, "Elsa, the true feminine, hitherto not understood by me, now understood at last."

With Elsa Wagner first realized that the "eternal feminine" lies not outside but within a man's soul. She is that feminine aspect within a man that he must acknowledge if he is to be a complete human being. She is especially important for an artist, for a man's inner feminine is the source of his creativity.

Then, in *The Flying Dutchman,* Wagner sets against his "eternal feminine" an archetypal male figure—the mysterious stranger, the pitiable monster, the beast with whom beauty is fascinated, the phantom lover. He is a figure from folk tale who can also be found in such novels by women as (to cite only the greatest ones) *Jane Eyre* and *Wuthering Heights.* He is often connected with the sea, for the sea is woman's great symbol of the unconscious. So in Ibsen's play *The Lady from the Sea* a woman cannot love the man she has married because once, at a lighthouse, she met a mysterious stranger in the mist who took her wedding ring and threw it with his into the water. In his many guises, this demon lover from the sea, this tormented Heathcliff fronting the storm on land, is a figure ever searching, and Wagner gives him this obsessive musical theme:

A less sinister appearance of this figure, and quite the best, at least to this classicist, comes in Homer's *Odyssey,* which is our oldest surviving combination of mythic archetypes and old sea stories. Wagner himself cited the *Odyssey* as a parallel to *The Flying Dutchman.* Some critics have found the *Odyssey* so feminine in its sensibility that they have suggested, not entirely fancifully, that it might have been composed by a woman in the age of Homer.

You'll remember the scene in the *Odyssey* in which the mysterious stranger meets the saving woman. Odysseus has been cast ashore in a storm. He has lost his ship and his crew. He is half dead with exhaustion, and naked except for the barnacles that cling to him and make him impossibly ugly. He has no idea whether he has landed among savages or civilized folk. But it is a morning of uncommon freshness, and the delectable princess Nausicaa is playing on the beach, tossing a ball to her serving maids. The cries of the girls at play startle Odysseus. For a moment he is afraid. Then, famous as he is for his pluck and his quick mind and his ability to come out ahead in any adventure, he resourcefully breaks off an olive branch to cover his nakedness and, as the serving girls flee, delicately meets the greatest challenge of his career—touching the heart of the chaste and inquisitive princess so that she will give him shelter. He guesses, correctly, that that very morning she wondered if she would ever meet the man who would be right for her. He doesn't tell her who he is, but he makes her feel that she is the only one who can save him. And she does.

The mysterious lover from the sea represents for a woman the strangely enchanted, frightening but pleadingly tender man who sees into her soul, and releases the creative instinct in her, though his background remains mysterious. So, in other Wagner pieces, Tannhäuser keeps his erotic past a secret from the chaste Elisabeth, Lohengrin withholds his name from the inquisitive Elsa, Siegmund comes as pseudonymously through the storm to Sieglinde as Tristan crosses to the sea to be healed by Isolde. Walther keeps a chaste distance from Eva, even though he has stayed overnight at her father's house, and approaches her discreetly in church. Parsifal does not even know his own name when he meets Kundry. All the Wagner heroes keep their past lives mysterious when they ask for acceptance from the women who really know them, need them, and help them.

The beginnings of these two Wagnerian figures, as old as Homer and wonderful archetypes for the male and the female, are in *The Flying Dutchman*. When for the first time Senta, the "eternal feminine," meets the Dutchman, the "mysterious lover," she screams a scream of instant recognition, and Wagner follows that with a long motionless silence in which the two look into each other's eyes with the realization that they have at last met their destinies. Freud and Jung have said nothing more about falling in love—finding in another what one most needs in oneself.

When the opera is seen in this way, as each lover fulfilled in the other, and each holding the other in a sort of mythic trance, Senta's ballad, at the center of the opera, assumes great importance. It is not just a narrative to explain the background of the story; it is nothing less than an incantation. Staring obsessively at the Dutchman's picture, and telling his story to repetitive rhythms, Senta conjures him up—much as Elsa does Lohengrin when she tells of her dream of him, and as the whisper of Elisabeth's name calls Tannnhäuser back to her. The Dutchman is summoned from the sea by Senta's inner desires. He does not, as we might expect, ask that Senta admit him into her world on land. Nor will she join him in his on the sea. Together they will create a world of their own. His redemption lies not in acceptance by any others, only in being accepted by her. And her salvation, once she has made her decision, lies nowhere but in fidelity to him. We last see them rising in the sun's rays over her forsaken harbor and his sunken ship. They have left their separate worlds behind, like Tristan and Isolde, like—to some degree—any two people completely in love.

The Flying Dutchman is a frightening opera, not just for its powerful evocation of elemental nature in its overture, not just for the remarkable confrontation of human and ghostly choruses in its penultimate scene, but for the hypnotic vision to which its lovers surrender. Years before the much more accomplished *Tristan, The Flying Dutchman* affirms with equal conviction the reality of an ecstatic state and the comparative unreality of day-to-day existence. It tells us what it is like to be in love: to be in love is to create a world more real for you than the everyday world, one inhabited only by you and the one you love. And *that,* this opera says, redeems you from all your inner demons.

The Flying Dutchman is the beginning of one of the most astonishing series of works ever created in any artistic medium. Ten operas that have held the stage for more than a hundred years and are, if anything, more popular now than ever before. Ten operas that, in ever-wider circles and at ever-increasing depth, tell much the same story. They are autobiographical works in which Wagner seeks to understand himself. But they are also, to the degree that we choose to see into them, our own works.

Works of art tell us about ourselves, and preserve for us experiences that otherwise would be lost to memory. Something of the wind and waves of that fjord at Sandwike has been captured in *The Flying Dutchman* forever. Something, too, of the ecstatic feeling any one of us has when falling in love. And something, finally, of a young composer's passionate need to be discovered, accepted, and understood, of his need to silence the demons that howled and the creative energies that endlessly bounded and surged within him.

YOU USE
WORKS OF ART
TO SEE YOUR
SOUL

Tannhäuser

If you had asked me in 1937 what my favorite music was, I would have said without hesitation, "Where or When," because at that time the harmonies in that song seemed wonderfully new and strange. But by 1938 I probably would have opted for "Love Walked In," especially for the harmonic change at the words "drove the shadows away." In 1939 I'd certainly have chosen the song everyone was singing that year, "Over the Rainbow," and in 1940 "All the Things You Are," with its subtle and lovely modulations. Those were radio days, and the golden age of American popular song. Month after month the new melodies came and went, each more beautiful in its harmonies than the last.

But the next year, all that changed for me. One Saturday afternoon, I heard my first opera broadcast from the Met, and nothing Richard Rodgers or George Gershwin or Harold Arlen or Jerome Kern had written meant to me what that new music did. That broadcast opera was *Tannhäuser*. Lauritz Melchior was singing, and also Astrid Varnay, Kerstin Thorborg,

Herbert Jannsen, and Alexander Kipnis. Erich Leinsdorf was conducting. Fifty years later I can still remember the sounds they made. The music simply swept over me like a tidal wave. Long after the broadcast was over, the new, strange, wonderful *Tannhäuser* harmonies were buzzing around in my head.

I'd had about a year of piano lessons at the time, from the Sisters of Charity in Detroit. During the depression my father had bought a player piano for ten dollars from a Polish family who were moving and couldn't get the big mahogany thing up the stairs. With the piano in the transaction came dozens of piano rolls (with Polish words next to the perforations), and a huge stack of sheet music. After the broadcast I headed for that stack. I knew that somewhere in it there was a dog-eared old book of opera pieces arranged for piano. And sure enough, there were several pages titled "Gems from *Tannhäuser*." I was just able to manage the shifting harmonies of the "Pilgrim's Chorus":

What a thrill it was, having under my young fingers the very sounds that were echoing in my head! It was something akin to Keats's first looking into Chapman's Homer. It was more than a discovery. It was a self-discovery. I felt that I had touched something that, however impossible it may sound in words, was a part of me. Something deep within me responded.

So there are two things you can say about *Tannhäuser* from the start. First, it is filled with the most astonishing harmonies—not so startling now as when they were first heard, perhaps, but still enough to shake an eleven-year-old boy off his musical groundings and change everything for him.

And second, *Tannhäuser,* for anyone who surrenders to its spell, tells something of one's own self—especially of one's young self. Eduard Hanslick, one day to be Wagner's severest critic, was only twenty-two when he attended the *Tannhäuser* premiere, in Dresden, at Wagner's personal invitation. He was overwhelmed, and wrote, in his first published article for his Viennese readers, that the opera was "a musical experience that carries the listener irresistibly along, so that what occurs in the orchestra and on the stage becomes a part of his life." Baudelaire was not so young—well into his thirties—when he first heard the *Tannhäuser* overture. But his response was much the same. "What I experienced was indescribable," he said. "It seemed to me I already knew this music. It seemed to me that it was my own music."

The young Wagner wrote that music quickly, and in later life said much the same as the rest of us about this young man's opera: "My whole being was consumed with it, so much so that I became obsessed with the thought that I was going to die before I completed it. And when I had set down the last note, I did feel as if my life had run its course."

Tannhäuser was of course not the end for Wagner. He went on to compose much more profound and disturbing dramas. And, for some people today, the once-forbidding *Tannhäuser* seems hopelessly dated and simplistic, a two-dimensional conflict between good and evil. Worse, it can seem an unconvincing victory of good *over* evil. And at this point in our century, when we are not so sure as we once were about many things, we reject moralizing oversimplifications, especially when they come in dramatic form.

But is *Tannhäuser* simplistic? It is set in a historical era of some complexity, at a time when a stable, nominally Christian society, confident of its political and spiritual values, was challenged by a renascent paganism, a new spirit that was drawing to itself the most creative elements in Christendom. It will help us to appreciate *Tannhäuser* if we see its hero as a man torn not so much between good and evil as between two worlds, two opposing sets of values, each of them essential to him.

One of the worlds is represented by Landgrave Hermann in his cliffed and commanding Wartburg, by the minnesingers with their chaste and courtly approach to the problems of human existence, and by the Thuringians with their sword-wielding moralizing. All of these represent the Middle Ages. The other world is the world of Venus, her open sensuality and her mythological following: naiads, sirens, nymphs, bacchants, satyrs, and fauns. These are an evocation of the Renaissance. The visions at the Venusberg—Leda and the swan, Europa and the bull, the three Graces linked arm in arm—are Renaissance pictures. The values that Tannhäuser draws from his experience in the Venusberg and then expresses in his songs at the Wartburg are similarly neopagan: one should put his hands and his lips to all that is beautiful, and not idealize it from afar. On one level, the opera is about a period in history in which everything is poised on the brink of change, and its hero, an artist, is the first to sense this. Small wonder the knights in the Wartburg draw their swords and the pope in Rome withholds his absolution. Tannhäuser's new paganism threatens the very foundations of the civilization they know.

The movement from medieval to Renaissance is one of the great moments in our history, and it was not effected without a struggle. The wonder of Wagner's opera is that he has caught the tension of that moment and centered it in the soul of his hero. His Tannhäuser is a man between two worlds, unable to rest in either. Cursed with insatiability by his pagan goddess, damned for eternity by his Christian pontiff, he struggles to understand himself after his soul has been wrenched apart. And eventually he achieves a synthesis of his two experiences—a synthesis the Western world strove for more than a century to achieve.

But *Tannhäuser* is still more than that. If we look beyond the period in which it is set, to the time in which it was composed, we can place it at another important moment in cultural history. Nineteenth-century German poets, looking for a kind of Renaissance in their day, sang that the gods of pagan antiquity had never died but had only passed beneath the earth, where they were still waiting to reveal themselves to any mortal who would seek them out and believe in them. "Schöne Welt, wo bist du?" was Schiller's question, set to music by Schubert: "Beautiful world, where are you?" Hölderlin saw his Germany awakening that world, rousing the gods of Greece from their centuries of slumber. Romanticism in Germany blended the medieval and the neopagan in a great rush of passionate feeling.

Wagner's questing hero is that sort of romantic: the pagan Christian seeking to know himself. Like that essential German mythic figure, Faust, Tannhäuser must have new experiences, he must search and strive, and sin so long as he strives, and win what Wagner always called "redemption" through the intercession of something we have already spoken of in connection with *The Flying Dutchman*—"das Ewig-Weibliche," the eternal feminine. That idea, immortalized in the last line of Goethe's *Faust* ("The eternal feminine leads us upward"), is the very essence of German romanticism: man may strive, through art and reason and physical force, toward a synthesis of human experience, but it is woman—or the feminine in man—who points his way to achieving it.

Wagner often quoted Goethe's last line, and Robert Donington, in his analysis of the *Ring,* says rightly, "If we cannot understand this final theme of redemption, we cannot understand Wagner. It was his lifelong preoccupation." Wagner was in fact writing an essay on the feminine principle in man when he died.

Elisabeth, then, is more important in *Tannhäuser* than we may at first have thought. It is often said that Elisabeth serves as a foil for Venus in the drama. But surely the Virgin Mary is the figure to set against Venus—the sacred set against the profane, the medieval against the Renaissance. Elisabeth is a central character, as central as Tannhäuser himself. She comes to know something of both his worlds—the sacred through her Christian faith, the new paganism through Tannhäuser's songs. She confesses in the second act that those songs brought to her "a strange new life . . . emotions I never felt before, longings I had never known." Wolfram says that Tannhäuser's songs have cast some sort of spell over her. She herself admits, in her last-act prayer, that she has had to struggle with the new, disturbing feelings.

Then she ascends to the Wartburg to die. Like so many deaths in Wagner, Elisabeth's comes of no physical cause and must be taken symbolically. Wagner's comment in the text is "Her path leads to heaven where she has an exalted mission to perform." She has the mission of the women who, at the end of Goethe's poem, bring Faust's striving soul to heaven. That is to say, she will lead her beloved spouse upward till the struggling elements within him have been reconciled.

The opera ends with two deaths and two symbols. First, Elisabeth dies, and the evening twilight is pierced by a star—appropriately enough, for Elisabeth has been likened to a star throughout the opera. I think, however, that the evening star can mean something more than is usually made of it. (Wagner's intuition at the close of his operas invariably surfaces in

expressive symbols.) What we call the evening star is an ambivalent symbol; it is both the planet Venus and, in the morning, she whom medieval Christians called the "stella matu-
tina," the Virgin Mary. Donington would call the star, with its
two opposed associations, a symbol of psychic wholeness, and
regard its appearance at the moment of Elisabeth's death as an
indication that she has, with feminine insight, reconciled the
two worlds her beloved still struggles with—Venus and the
Virgin. Now she will light the way for him.

Then Tannhäuser dies, again of no physical causes, and new
pilgrims arrive from Rome carrying the pope's staff, which is
blossoming with green leaves. The symbolism here is Christian, from Wagner's medieval sources, but we should not limit
its application to Christianity. In fact, Wagner dismissed
"those critics who insist on reading into my *Tannhäuser* a specifically Christian meaning, and a pietistic one at that." What
we have, again, is a sign that opposing values have been reconciled. The greening of the papal scepter is the hero's symbol,
as the star is the heroine's. Conflicting ideals have been syn-
thesized: medieval Christendom has accepted the values of the
new Renaissance paganism.

Ultimately in Wagner it is the music that should explain the
symbol, and Wagner does not disappoint us here. Just as the
papal staff has sprouted leaves, so Wagner's Christian hymn,
the "Pilgrim's Chorus," is surrounded at the close by the puls-
ing music of paganism:

As the composer himself explains, "The music of the Venusberg sounds amid the hymn of God. Two forces, the spiritual

and the sensual, are united." That was anticipated in Act I by that Tannhäuser-in-miniature, the little shepherd boy. In the valley between the two worlds of Venusberg and Wartburg, he sings of the figure from German folklore who represents both Venus and the Virgin: Frau Holde, who leads the singer upward from the mountain fastness to a flowering landscape.

Tannhäuser is not, then, a simple dramatization of the victory of sacred over profane, of spirit over flesh, of Christianity over paganism. It is a celebration of a synthesis of those opposites, the healing of a soul torn between two worlds.

Who are we reminded of in all of this? Well, so long as we are in Germany at the beginnings of the Renaissance, Tannhäuser should remind us of another tormented young protester who was gifted in song, clashed with the pope, sought refuge in the Wartburg, defied the society he knew, and profoundly changed it. Did Wagner have Martin Luther in mind as he wrote?

Or is Wagner's hero a projection of himself? The young composer of *Tannhäuser* was, like his hero, soon to stop at the Wartburg on his way to political exile with a price on his head. He was soon to act out his own scenario. He would be scorned and attacked for his new music. He would shock the bourgeoisie with his scandalous sex life. He would be driven by the demon in him to sing ever more fervid stories of neopagan redemption—a musician unable to win a hearing because of his unorthodoxy, a romantic insisting that sexuality be experienced and not idealized, a social outcast at a state of awareness beyond that of his contemporaries. In the contest of nineteenth-century music, Schumann and Brahms, like the singers at the Wartburg, could not understand him. Only Liszt, a trusty Wolfram, would take his part. But what could even Liszt know of the fires that consumed him? Fortunately, there would be a series of Elisabeths to help him through his crises. In short, Wagner was to be the Tannhäuser of his time.

"All very well," say those who reject the opera, "but does *Tannhäuser* make any sense in *our* time?"

It most surely does. For a production in Houston in the early seventies I wrote a piece about Tannhäuser's being a figure for the troubled romantics of that era—openly protesting, at odds with themselves and with authority, obsessed with sex, flaunting their psychedelic experiences in violent new musical styles. It was easy, on a university campus, to relate *Tannhäuser* to the cult film of those times, *A Clockwork Orange,* and back to Baudelaire, who described his reactions to the opera in terms that clearly refer to the effects of opium and hashish.

But that era is now past, and *Tannhäuser* continues to speak. Its hero is anyone who reaches a level of awareness that makes it impossible for him to return to his older, simpler, more innocent ways. It speaks for anyone who has ever had to relate a whole new world of intellectual or spiritual or sensual revelations to the older, traditional values of the world in which he is placed. Most of us who love music or art or literature or philosophy have had, at some time in our lives, to struggle through that sort of crisis. Perhaps we came through it only with the help of someone who loved us and led us upward out of our despair. *Tannhäuser* shows us a soul undergoing that experience.

When I first struck those *Tannhäuser* chords on that ten–dollar piano, it was not just the discovery of the harmonies that thrilled me. It was the self-discovery. When the tormented Baudelaire first heard those harmonies, he wrote Wagner to say, "Thank you. You have shown me the way back to myself."

Will we still need *Tannhäuser* in the next century? George Bernard Shaw, in a play set in the year 31920, says, "You use a glass mirror to see your face; you use works of art to see your soul." If he is right, and I think he is, *Tannhäuser* we shall always need.

ONE

BRIEF SHINING
MOMENT

Lohengrin

If you've ever been to Switzerland—and what American, given a chance to go to Europe, doesn't visit Switzerland?— you'll have seen widely advertised as one of the excursions the trip to the Rigi. Wagner took his first wife, Minna, on that trip one day in 1850. It was the day on which *Lohengrin* was being given its first performance, far, far away in Weimar. They couldn't be there, and she cried (partly because she knew he'd been unfaithful), and they both needed something by way of a reconciliation. So up to the Rigi they went. And from the top of the mountain it was as if they could see all the world.

Wagner was in exile in Switzerland. Minna had come to join him there. A few years before, in Dresden, she'd pleaded with him not to get politically involved. But how could he not— this hotheaded young German? He was excited about the possibility of his divided Germany coming together. He was every bit as excited as, south of the Alps, another composer almost exactly his age was excited about the possibility of his divided Italy coming together. There, Verdi's name had become a symbol of revolt, and he wrote opera after opera about the Italian resurgence. In Germany Wagner wrote *Lohengrin* and became actively involved in the revolutionary uprising in Dresden, providing ammunition, making inflammatory speeches, dodging bullets as he kept watch from the tower of the Kreuzkirche. He was sure, back then, that a new Germany was being born. No wonder an important part of his new *Lohengrin* told how King Henry the Fowler once traveled the length and breadth of German-speaking lands in an attempt to unite them.

But the revolution in Dresden failed, *Lohengrin* remained unperformed, and Wagner had to flee Germany. Some of his fellow revolutionaries were captured and sentenced to death—though eventually the sentences were commuted to long prison terms. Wagner, with forged papers and an assumed name, found refuge in Zurich. There he wrote no music for almost six years. Instead, in a stream of prose writings, he started rethinking his ideas about politics, music, drama, and much besides. When he broke his long musical silence with the first notes of the *Ring,* he was a wholly different composer, and a very great one.

Some Wagnerites will not bother themselves with anything Wagner wrote before that first E-flat of the *Ring.* But Wagner himself longed, while the *Ring* music was shaping in him, to hear *Lohengrin*—*Lohengrin,* with its hope for German unity and its hero who was so much an idealization of his young self. He sent the score to Franz Liszt in Weimar, and pleaded with him to get it on the stage.

Liszt, always willing to help other men of genius, complied. And on the day of the premiere, Wagner, far away in Switzerland, took Minna up to the Rigi. And there, in the mountains, he was, like an Old Testament prophet, confirmed in his mission by a sign. On the Rigi there sometimes occurs a natural phenomenon called the Rigi specter. It occurred that day as the sun set. Wagner, who loved mountains and loved taking risks, walked to the edge of the abyss, and saw a giant reflection of himself cast across the misty sky over the towering peaks. His head was haloed in light. So he knew, this little man with titanic dreams, that hundreds of miles beyond the Alps, *Lohengrin,* his romantic opera on German unity, would be a success, and that his plans for a new work, eventually to be four operas on the nature of the world itself, would also come to realization.

Twelve more years passed before Wagner heard his *Lohengrin.* As the time of exile wore on and *Lohengrin* was performed in his absence all over Germany, Wagner said, pleased with his success but laughing in his pain, that he just might be the only German who had never heard it. When an orchestra was assembled in Zurich to give a concert of his music, and Wagner, conducting the rehearsals, actually heard for the first time his own *Lohengrin* prelude, with the absolutely new sound of the A-major eight-part string writing, he wrote to Liszt, "I had to get a good grip on myself not to break down."

What he finally heard for himself, and what forever after the greatest orchestrators were to marvel at, was an astonishing use of orchestral textures to suggest color. A major is almost invariably thought a bright key. Mozart loved it. It suggested the gleam of gold, or perhaps shining silver. Yet Wagner, dividing his first and second violins each into four parts, and setting them to play in the upper reaches of their registers, makes this traditionally bright key suggest the soft, clear, blue expanses of the sky:

A vision of the Holy Grail begins to form in that ethereal blue, and the music passes almost imperceptibly from A into E major and then, as the sacred cup appears in its full glory, into D major—all keys associated, again, with brightness. D major is certainly right for the full revelation of the burnished, blazing Grail, and at that moment we get brass, and a full orchestra. But the wonder of the prelude is how, before that, Wagner's divided strings change the effect of these predominantly sharp keys, turning them ethereally soft. Blue is the *Lohengrin* color. Thomas Mann spoke lovingly of the prelude's "blausilberne Schönheit," its "silvery blue beauty." Baudelaire said that it held him suspended in a preternatural state, "in an ecstasy compounded of joy and insight."

Perhaps Baudelaire, with a poet's perception, sensed then that *Lohengrin* was not just a romantic tale of knighthood in flower, not just a patriotic call for the unification of Germany, but something for all times and places, that *Lohengrin* was about the soul. In recent years, we've come to see the *Ring* that way, as taking place within the human psyche—its rivers and forests the landscape of the unconscious, its storms and calms our inner emotions, with Wotan as consciousness and Brünnhilde as will and Loge as instinct and Erda as intuition. Wagner himself said as much. In an attempt to explain what he was doing in the *Ring,* Wagner said, long before Freud, that it was the purpose of art "to make the unconscious conscious."

There are intimations of this kind of drama in *The Flying Dutchman,* and still more in *Tannhäuser.* But in *Lohengrin* we really begin to feel that Wagner is moving into a new kind of drama, in which the contents of the psyche are made visible. *Lohengrin,* set in a historically detailed Antwerp, nonetheless suggests much more than that time and place. Its characters are more than personages of history and legend. They are figures of myth. If you have ever seen *Lohengrin,* you must have noticed that, though Ortrud is on stage all through Act I, she says nothing; she expresses her secret thoughts only in the ensembles. Telramund does all the talking for her. She is in a strange sort of reciprocal relationship with him. He speaks; she is silent. But there is no question that she is the strong one. He is her public spokesman, her public agent, no more. He is slain the moment her end is achieved. He is dispensible. She seduced him for her ends, and willed him to be what he became. They are an interesting pair—destructive forces operating interdependently, he the outer, she the inner one.

There is an even more interesting reciprocal relationship between Lohengrin and Elsa, something truly mythic. When Wagner tried to explain Lohengrin and Elsa to his friends, he used the myth of Zeus and Semele. The Greek sky god Zeus left his Olympian light to love the mortal woman Semele, and in the darkness she asked him to reveal himself openly, in all his glory. He had told her never to ask that of him, but ask she did, and to show his love for her, he came to Semele in all his thunder and light. And the full sight of him killed her.

Like most myths, that is about the human psyche. Man and woman, Wagner said, are like two parts of the soul. He is consciousness, brightness and light. She is the unconscious, the dark intuitive. Each fulfills the longings of the other. The young, politically oriented Wagner identified with the man when he wrote *Lohengrin*. Later, writing the *Ring,* he looked back on *Lohengrin* and saw that the woman was part of him too, and an essential part of him—his questioning intuition, the true source of his creativity. "Elsa," he exclaimed, "Elsa, the unconscious, the intuitive, in whom Lohengrin's consciousness longs to be fulfilled. Elsa, the true feminine, who can save me, and the world. Elsa, the feminine, hitherto not understood by me, now understood at last."

Ernest Newman, at this point, said, "Well who, in the name of heaven, takes Lohengrin and Elsa so seriously as that?" Andrew Porter responded, rightly, "Wagner did." Wagner was clearly moving on to Brünnhilde, the questioning, intuitive, saving woman of the *Ring*. And he was strikingly anticipating twentieth-century psychiatry, wherein the human person seeks wholeness, integration, and union between consciousness (the male principle) and the unconscious (the female principle). With *Lohengrin* and the *Ring,* Wagner began to realize what he was doing in his art. He was "making the unconscious conscious." He was mapping out that lost continent that lies deep in the soul, the world we usually experience in dreams or know from myths.

Perhaps all of this began for Wagner musically when he wrote the first mysterious page of *Lohengrin*'s Act II, and introduced the serpentine theme of the tempter Ortrud:

and the theme of the forbidden question, "Nie sollst du mich befragen" ("That you must never ask me"):

The forbidden question, the breaking of an imposed taboo, is a familiar motif in myth. It is in the myth of Semele, as Wagner reminds us. It is also in the myth of Psyche, the beautiful princess whose very name means "soul." In the darkness Psyche lit a lamp and looked on her lover, though he had told her not to, and she lost him. (She also opened a jar she had brought up from the world of the dead and was told not to look into, and its perfumes sent her into a deathly sleep.) And then there is the first woman in Greek myth, Pandora, whose name means "all gifts." She was given a box and told not to open it. But she did, and found it was filled with all evils. It was she who brought evil into the world.

And what, along with the breaking of the imposed taboo, have all of these stories of disobedient women in common? Instant sorrow, but ultimate good. For when Semele is destroyed, her unborn child is rescued: he is Dionysus, irrational god of the dark unconscious. And when Psyche is wakened from her sleep, her lover makes her immortal: he is Eros, irrational god of sexual passion. And when Pandora unleashes all the evils on the world, one last winged creature is left inside the box, after all the others have flown away: it is Elpis, the spirit of hope.

Instant sorrow, ultimate good.

The Judaeo-Christian tradition has the most famous of these taboo-breaking women: Eve. She eats of the fruit of the tree of the knowledge of good and evil, which she was told not to do, and so she ends, for herself and for her Adam, a life of preternatural bliss. She brings immediate sorrow to herself and suffering to all her descendants. But the church in its liturgy sings that ultimately the disobedience was a "felix culpa," a "happy fault," because it began the whole wonderful plan of redemption, and brought us eventually "talem Redemptorem," a redeemer in Jesus.

I think mythologists agree, and I think all but the most fundamentalist religious writers agree, that these taboo-breaking stories describe a great evolutionary moment in human prehistory, when the human race passed from a blissful state of unconsciousness, a state when man lived only through instinct, to the much more problematic state of consciousness, when reason emerged, and man started to think, and to know what was good and what was evil. At first it may have seemed a catastrophe, a tragic loss. Ultimately it was a triumph. "You will become like gods," was the message the serpent tempter gave to Eve, and he was right. Man evolved, emerged into a state where, like God, he could know—fully conscious, but with his psyche still rooted in the unconscious.

Now here's something we might well ponder. Aren't the taboos in myth meant to be broken? When God put the tree in the Garden of Eden and told his man and woman not to eat of it, didn't he know they would? Couldn't he have planned it, so that they would evolve? We have traditionally called the disobedience of Adam and Eve a sin, the "original sin." Humankind's myths have always felt guilt about that first perception of good and evil. The breakthrough to consciousness, the new awareness of the ambivalent potential that lies within the human soul, is a rueful memory. It meant losing innocence, breaking the bond with nature, acquiring consciousness of what separates the human race from the rest of creation. But the gain was, in all the myths that tell of it, greater than the loss. And if it is the woman—Eve, Pandora, Semele, Psyche —who takes the evolutionary step first, it is not because she is the more frail. It is because she is the more intuitive. She knows intuitively that the step must be taken. Then, despite immediate loss, there will be, ultimately, progress.

Elsa has often been thought a wan and witless heroine. I hope that she is beginning to seem more important in the scheme of things in *Lohengrin*.

And now we should look, at last, to *Lohengrin*'s most eloquent symbol: the swan. The mythmakers of the Dark and Middle Ages, the best intuitors in our Western tradition, introduced the swan into their version of the woman-breaking-the-taboo myth. It is clearly meant to be significant. What do our specialists in symbols say about the swan?

Jacques de Morgan, in his *L'Humanité Préhistorique,* notes that in many mythologies spirited horses pull the chariot of the sun across the sky by day, but it is the swan that draws the sun under the world by night. Gaston Bachelard, in *L'Eau et les Rêves,* sees the swan as signifying the integration of male and female principles. And J. E. Cirlot, in his *Símboles Tradicionales,* says that in medieval alchemy the swan was the harbinger of change, of transformation. All three of these associations—an unconscious underlying consciousness, an integration there of male and female principles, a transformation—fit with our observations so far.

Finally, Carl Jung, the most important interpreter of symbols for our time, and so often the most helpful in interpreting Wagner, sees the swan in myth as a transcendence symbol, a symbol that bears witness to the existence of a world beyond the world we know. Wagner gives his swan a two-note motif.

Just the wave of a graceful wing, or the wail of a sad song. It falls:

That swan motif actually comes out of the opening music of the prelude. When in the soft blue a vision of the Grail begins to form, the swan motif is there:

Wagner uses the swan and its motif again in his other opera about the Holy Grail, *Parsifal*. The swan is a symbol of the Grail's power, of the existence of a transcendent world that can, in a moment of grace, touch us in our troubled world.

What does the swan in *Lohengrin* mean? On a historical level, it is a sign from outside history that the German nations may now move toward a transformation, toward unity and integration. On an autobiographical level (always an aspect of Wagner's work), the swan is a symbol for Wagner's art, which brings his intuitive insights to us who listen. But on the deepest, mythic level, the swan is a symbol that the human soul, the real stage on which *Lohengrin* is played, can be transformed. It is witness to the existence of a power beyond the soul that can touch it and transform it, though some happy fault may be needed to bring about the evolutionary progress.

I won't say that this is all that the swan means, for myths are always wiser than any interpretations drawn from them. But it is clear that transformations are at work, quickly, with the transformation of the swan at the close of *Lohengrin*. Lohengrin leaves and Elsa dies; her asking the forbidden question brings instant sorrow. But it also brings ultimate good: Ortrud's power deserts her, and young Gottfried appears, like Dionysus, or Eros, or Elpis, or Jesus, to be the hope for the future. The chorus sings, as its last words, "Sorrow, sorrow," but the orchestra, with the omniscience that Wagner's orchestra was to have forever after, plays the Grail motif *without the swan in it,* for a transcendent power has worked the needed transformation. On the last page the Grail theme does not fall. With a simple chord progression it lifts to a final, silver-blue chord.

Nine out of ten plot synopses will tell you that it was Ortrud who changed the young Gottfried into a swan. But if you look at Wagner's text carefully, you will see that Ortrud recognizes that the swan is Gottfried only when she sees the chain with which she enchanted the boy still hanging on the swan's neck. She made the boy disappear. But was it she who turned him into a swan? In Wagner's sources it is a power for good that preserves young princes as swans. In Wagner's music it seems clear that it was the Grail that saved the boy from Ortrud, and sent him back in the symbolic form of a swan to the land he would one day lead.

Many a storybook prince, like Camelot's King Arthur, is metamorphosed into a bird or beast, to be preserved for a time from harm and to learn, from his experience in the animal kingdom, how to govern his people when he grows up and becomes king. It's a romantic idea, and it appealed powerfully to a romantic young king who didn't know how to govern but wished he did, who wasn't chaste but longed to be, who loved *Lohengrin* and built swan castles, even a lake with a swan boat in it, to externalize his longings. Perhaps that king, Ludwig II of Bavaria, should have the last say on *Lohengrin*. He knew that the swan was a transcendence symbol, and no king wanted to find a transcendent world to help him more than he did.

All the same, I'll save the last say for myself. I love *Lohengrin*. When I see or hear it, I'm with Wagner on some precipice, and I see myself projected against a blue sky. Like Baudelaire, I'm suspended in a preternatural state blended of ecstasy and insight. I can sense that there is a world that transcends this one and, in one brief shining moment, it can touch me. I can sense too that I am made to be more than I am. There are transformations that can still be worked in me. In my consciousness and my intuition, in my masculine and my feminine. Even if I fail, all is not lost. Truly human failings can be happy faults. And at the end of all is an A-major silvery blue beauty.

Maybe that's a fairytale vision, a romantic nineteenth-century vision, a false vision, of reality. But there are twentieth-century thinkers who would not say so. Wagner intuited the mythic truth in this romantic tale from centuries past. And as we have discovered in our own century, myths are about what happens or can happen within all of us. Within all of us, *Lohengrin* happens. On the landscape of the soul.

SONGBIRDS
AND
SAINTS

Die Meistersinger

To say anything about *Die Meistersinger* requires a superlative of some sort. It is, for one thing, the longest opera in the standard repertory—at least, according to *The Guinness Book of Records,* where Reginald Goodall's performance clocks in at five hours and fifteen minutes, exclusive of intermissions. And the overture to *Die Meistersinger* has been, over the years, the most often performed piece of music in North American concert halls—at least, according to annual trade figures from BMI. *Die Meistersinger* can also lay claim to having "the greatest libretto ever written"—at least, according to Patrick J. Smith, author of that authoritative study of librettos, *The Tenth Muse.*

But many Wagnerites at Bayreuth will use a superlative from the other end of the scale. They say that *Die Meistersinger* is the least of all the Master's works, "too diatonic" or "too Christian" or "too German" or even "too shallow" or otherwise uncharacteristic of the Master.

Accordingly, with those whom we may call non-Wagnerites, *Die Meistersinger* is often cited as Wagner's one relatively healthy product, a sort of anomalous accident, and quite the (superlative) "most acceptable" of his works.

Finally, there are those of us who, when pressed, would use a more personal sort of superlative: favorite. We would give *Die Meistersinger* pride of place in any roll call of works for the musical stage. And we're not all of us Germans. Among our number are the Englishman John Culshaw, who spoke so eloquently during the Metropolitan Opera broadcast intermissions; the Italian Arturo Toscanini, who wanted to lay his baton down finally only after conducting *Die Meistersinger;* and the Polish patriot, composer, and pianist Ignacy Jan Paderewski, who cited *Die Meistersinger* as "the greatest work of genius ever achieved by any artist in any field."

Superlative it may be, but my favorite opera had pretty humble beginnings. The idea of writing it first came to Wagner when he was a young man, in the summer of 1845. On his doctor's advice, he took a cure at Marienbad, the famous spa in Bohemia. He was under orders to do no writing. The weather was glorious, and he had a good book to read—*Parzifal,* by Wolfram von Eschenbach, a poet he had just put on the stage, as a baritone, in *Tannhäuser.* Wolfram would make nice, relaxing reading in the woods and by the streams.

But, as almost anyone could confidently predict, Wagner got excited when he started to read Wolfram's *Parzifal,* and the related legends of Parzifal's son, Lohengrin. Two potential operas started welling up in Wagner so urgently that, to distract himself, he turned to another book, on the history of German literature. And before long he was drafting, out of that, a third potential opera. Just a little thing, really, about the old mastersingers of Nuremberg. Only a comedy, so his doctor couldn't really object to his writing it down, could he? Besides, it would put all of Wolfram's romantic knights, those Parzifals and Lohengrins, out of his head for a while. It could be performed, this little comedy, as a diversion after festive performances of the three acts of his new *Tannhäuser*. It would be like the little satyr play that followed the three festive tragedies in a day of drama in classic Athens. And it would fit nicely with his *Tannhäuser,* which was about the minnesingers of the Wartburg. This would be about the mastersingers of Nuremberg.

Well, Wagner was settling into his bath at Marienbad one afternoon when Wolfram's knights came back to him with a vengeance and, as he records, he leapt out of the bath and hardly stopped to pull on his clothes before he got back to his room. The text of *Lohengrin* had to be got down on paper. Then, as his doctor gave up on him, the music of the love duet of *Lohengrin* started to form in the margin of the text. After that, through *Lohengrin* and revolution and flight and political exile and endless prose writings and stormy love affairs, Wagner wrote *Das Rheingold* and *Die Walküre* and most of *Siegfried* and all of *Tristan und Isolde,* and finally, almost twenty years after the idea first came to him, he produced *Die Meistersinger von Nürnberg.* All along it had been growing within him, from a tiny little sketch to the mightiest of his operas.

He wrote the text in Paris, where, as always, his rejection and disappointment filled him with an intense longing for all things German: the art of Dürer, the tales of Hoffmann, the winding streets of old Nuremberg, and the cobbler poet Hans Sachs who once lived there. The story shaped itself almost like a fairy tale. A knight in shining armor comes to Nuremberg to rescue a maiden in distress—not with a sword but with a song. The maiden's father, who loves music with all his heart, has rather unwisely put her up as the prize in a singing competition, and it looks as if she will be carried off by a ridiculous dragon of a fellow named Beckmesser. But, with only one day to go, our knight defeats that dragon and rescues that maiden. But he needs wise old Hans Sachs to help him.

It's a comedy, all right, but I don't think it has been re-marked how very much in the mainstream of comedy it is. If you've ever seen *A Funny Thing Happened on the Way to the Forum*, you may know that our comic tradition in the West goes back twenty-two centuries, to the Roman comedians Plautus and Terence—and even twenty-four centuries, to the Athenian Menander and what was called, in the fourth century B.C., "New" Comedy. In all of those old comedies we meet, in play after play, these characters:

the *adolescens*, the inexperienced young hero who has only till morning to win his girl, and who is lectured at from all sides (Wagner's young knight, Walther);

the *servus*, the experienced slave who does most of the lecturing but gets into a lot of trouble himself (Wagner's apprentice, David);

the *mulier*, the girl who is going to be given away in the morning (Wagner's Eva);

the *nutrix*, the confidante who tries to help the boy get the girl (Wagner's Magdalene);

the *senex*, the philosophizing older man, often secretly in love with the girl himself (Wagner's central figure, Hans Sachs);

the *leno*, the procurer who puts the girl up for sale (con-siderably softened by Wagner as Eva's music-loving fa-ther, Pogner); and

the *miles gloriosus*, the ridiculously overconfident braggart soldier, who hopes to get the girl in the morning (whom

Shakespeare used as a model for Falstaff, but who appears even more visibly as Wagner's Beckmesser).

I mention all of this not because I'm a professor of classics or to imply that Wagner's comedy is unduly derivative but to place *Die Meistersinger* where it deserves to be placed: in the great comic tradition of the West, a tradition that reaches from Greek Menander to the Romans, to Renaissance Italy, to Lope de Vega in a hundred Spanish comedies, to Shakespeare in *The Tempest,* Molière in *Les Fourberies de Scapin,* and Beaumarchais, Mozart, and Rossini in the Figaro plays. Of all of those postclassical works, *Die Meistersinger* is, I think, truest to classic type. And yet, *mirabile dictu,* the plot and characters seem perfectly at home transferred to sixteenth-century Germany.

I suspect that Wagner availed himself of the most traditional of plots, with the most typical of characters, because he wanted a solid base for what was going to be, on one level, an autobiographical manifesto. In his opera Wagner casts himself as the young knight, Walther. And the Mastersingers who oppose Walther are the critics who had opposed Wagner for some thirty years. And Beckmesser, called Hans Lich in an early draft of the libretto, is beyond much doubt the Viennese music critic Eduard Hanslick. And the central figure, Hans Sachs, represents the whole German tradition in art and music: the historical Hans Sachs first, but also Luther and Bach and Goethe and all the great figures to Beethoven. In the course of his opera, Wagner uses Hans Sachs to show that long German tradition marveling at Wagner's music and fighting for it, as a new and true expression of the best in the past.

The opera is more complicated than that because Hans Sachs often speaks for the mature Wagner too. One of the many astonishing things about *Die Meistersinger* is how the little

Greek and Roman plot blossoms, in Wagner's shaping imagination, into a dramatic structure of cathedralesque proportions.

And the music? That blossoms too. "It is my finest work," Wagner said as he composed. "I weep and I laugh over it." He worked at it with the song-filled quickness of a Mozart, a Schubert. He found a dedicated young man named Hans Richter, a horn player in the Vienna Opera orchestra, who was willing to live with him and his family on Lake Lucerne. (Later of course Richter was to become a famous conductor.) In a room over Wagner's, Richter copied sheet after sheet of the immense score as it was passed up to him. And he wondered: Wagner was scoring for virtually the same orchestra as Beethoven had used in the Fifth Symphony, with only three additional brass players and a harp added. Yet how wondrously new was the orchestral effect! It was altogether different from *Lohengrin*'s silver-blue beauty, and the *Ring*'s sounding rivers and forests, and *Tristan*'s feverish, surging chromaticism. Here all was a rich, mellow, diatonic C-major ripeness, the old and the new effortlessly combined.

Liszt played through the entire piano score in a single evening, exclaiming over and over on its beauty. Hans von Bülow, preparing for the first performance, wrote to a friend, "You cannot begin to imagine its wealth of music, the Cellini-workmanship in every detail. Wagner is the greatest composer, the equal of Beethoven and Bach, and more besides."

We can understand that enthusiasm. Wagner's friends were watching the creation of a great work of art, and there is nothing so thrilling as that. Has there been anything so thrilling on the Broadway stage in recent years as the scene in *Sunday in the Park with George* where, before our very eyes, the pointillist painter Georges Seurat creates his masterpiece, "La Grande Jatte"? It's a magic moment in the theater, but no more magical than the corresponding moment in Wagner's opera when, in his workshop, Hans Sachs helps Walther create, out of the memory of a dream, a master song, as we watch and listen.

We're about four hours into the opera by that time, and we're just beginning to sense something really wonderful about it—something Alfred Lorenz first pointed out and Boris Goldovsky once explained during one of these intermissions. Halfway through the third act, we begin to feel instinctively that every note, every bar of this great work is exactly in place. And why do we feel that? Because we've been told, by Hans Sachs and by young David and by the Mastersingers themselves, that in a master song there must be two stanzas, or *Stollen,* of identical length, each with the same melody, and with a rhyme at the end. And then, as a kind of resolution, there has to be an aftersong, an *Abgesang,* as long as the two *Stollen* together, with a wholly new melody.

Through Acts I and II and the first part of Act III, we've heard several attempts at this—from Walther and David and Beckmesser—and now it's becoming increasingly clear, to our amazement, that Act I and Act II have been approximately the same length, and that there are several incidents and even some bits of dialogue in Act I that are paralleled in Act II, and that each act ends with a sort of rhyme in the story—public rioting over what is judged bad music.

In other words, Acts I and II are two *Stollen.* And Act III is an *Abgesang*—as long as the first two acts together, with a new strain of seriousness, and a harmonious resolution. The whole opera is one immense master song. The whole of *Die Meistersinger*—shaping itself before our very ears—is Wagner's answer to his critics, a song offered them to meet *their* specifications, filled with all the things *they* demanded from and found wanting in his other work: diatonic structures, counterpoint, singable tunes, ensembles, folk dances worthy of Weber and chorales worthy of Bach, and, above all, thoroughly human characters.

And here, with human characters, I'll make my final observation in this intermission. What moves me most about *Die Meistersinger* is the humanity of Hans Sachs. He is, in fact, a model for me. He is an educator who teaches not just rules and techniques but how to think and feel. He loves music as much as he loves his chosen profession, and he sees the connection between the two. He is a celibate whose true children are those whose lives he touches and enriches. He is the good man I would like to be—helping Walther to shape his intuitive inspirations, guiding Eva generously and wisely in her unfolding love for Walther, teaching David his trade and, at the same time, opening him up to wider issues, opposing Beckmesser because Beckmesser can destroy the happiness of the others. And besides, Beckmesser has a lot to learn.

But Sachs, like all the great characters in opera, also learns. He comes to see deeply into life, to accept its inevitable limitations, and to embrace it fully. He is a character that a man, when he doubts and fails and prays and wonders, can want to identify with, and grow with.

At the end of a performance of *Die Meistersinger,* we in the audience are proud to the point of cheering that humankind can triumph over its tragic flaws and produce out of its sorrows great, laughing works of art. I can remember leaving performances of other Wagner operas walking on air, and turned wonderingly inward. But after *Die Meistersinger,* filled with at least as much emotion, I am turned outward. I want to embrace all the world. After some performances, as I left the theater, Munich or Zurich, London or New York seemed transformed—and not just by some midsummer moon or midwinter snow. There was something essentially right with the world. Life made sense. Life was in fact brimful of meaning, and I was eager to live it.

That's what great art can mean. Maybe that's why people speak of *Die Meistersinger* in superlatives.

II

When I went to the movies as a boy, there would often be a big storybook up there on the screen, and some unseen hand would pull it open, and the pages would start turning by themselves, and then I'd be swept into the story. That is what *Die Meistersinger* is in my mind's eye: a big illuminated manuscript, a massive medieval songbook, with secular and sacred melodies jostling each other page after page for hundreds and hundreds of pages. Some unseen hand pulls the book open at the first chord of the overture, and then the pages turn of themselves, and the melodies pour out in wondrous profusion, and the irresistible onward movement through the pages keeps me breathless, through all the designs and devices, the crotchets and demisemiquavers, the illuminations and recapitulations, the shining images, the pain and laughter and wisdom of it all, till the last page echoes the first.

I use a metaphor to describe *Die Meistersinger* because *Die Meistersinger* itself is filled with metaphors. Just about everything in it, large and small, is or means something else. And one of the pleasures of hearing it again and again is the thrill of discovering again what else and what else and what else it all means.

The moment the curtain rises, on the last chord of the overture, the metaphors begin to work. The people of Nuremberg are in church, just finishing a vesper hymn to John the Baptist: "Once our Savior came to thee, / By thy hand baptized to be."

They sing in the style of a Lutheran chorale, but their sacred song:

is a musical variant of the secular tune that opens the opera:

So right from the start it should be clear that in this opera, the sacred will be a metaphor for the secular. The entire action takes place on the eve and feast of a saint—the saint to whom the Savior himself came for baptism, Saint John the Baptist. Why did Wagner choose, of all days, that day?

Let's say, first, that Saint John's day, Johannistag, June 24, is a Christian feast superimposed on the old pagan observance of the summer solstice. On the eve of that midsummer day, evil spirits were thought to fare abroad and make men mad until Saint John sent good spirits in the morning. It's the perfect day for Wagner's story, for both Acts I and II of *Die Meistersinger,* set on the eve of the feast, end with bursts of midsummer madness or, as Hans Sachs calls it, *Wahn.* Evil spirits are at work, like glowworms in the dark. Then, on the morning after, in Act III, a song comes out of a midsummer night's dream, and Hans Sachs uses it to banish Nuremberg's evil spirits, its "Poltergeister," and to conjure up good spirits, "Gute Geister."

There's another reason for using John the Baptist's day. That day gave us the very fundament of our music. The notes of our scale—ut, re, mi, fa, sol, la, ti, ut—weren't named first by Maria von Trapp. They were taken by Guido d'Arezzo from the opening syllables of each successive line of the old Latin hymn sung for centuries on John the Baptist's eve:

ut queant laxis

*re*sonare fibris

*mi*ra gestorum

*fa*muli tuorum

*sol*ve polluti

*la*bii reatum

San*cte* Johannes.

(When *ut* eventually proved a little flat, *do* was substituted, from Latin *Domine*.)

So, as Wagner begins his story, he has his townsfolk sing a German version of the Latin hymn to the Baptist that first gave us the notes of our scale. He wants us to know that, in *Die Meistersinger,* baptism will be a metaphor for music. And he fills his John-the-Baptist opera with scales, from the opening motif of the mastersingers to this statement of the rules for songwriting:

Let us turn now to a second pattern of metaphors. Anyone who follows the opera with a libretto will notice, through Act I, scores of references to songbirds. Walther is told he must learn such mastersinger tones as the "goldfinch," the "lark," and the "pelican." But he has his own kind of song, which he first learned in winter by the fireside in his castle, from an old book by another Walther, the famous Walther von der Vogelweide (that is to say, Walther of the Bird Meadow). And he learned still more in the spring, from the meadow birds themselves. So he is impatient with the masters, though they bear such names as Nachtigall (nightingale) and Vogelgesang (bird song), and even the master who is sick and can't be there is named Niklaus Vogel (Nicholas the bird). In his trial song, Walther likens himself to a bird that soars above such owls, rooks, magpies, and crows. No wonder the masters reject him! They know something about metaphor, too.

And so the bird references continue, through Acts II and III, to the last scene, when all of Nuremberg rises to greet Hans Sachs with the chorale "Wacht auf!": "Awake! The dawn is drawing near, and in the green wood I hear a nightingale." The historical Sachs wrote those words in the sixteenth century, and had Martin Luther in mind. But such is the cumulative richness of association in the opera that when we hear the words in Act III, we think, "Yes, the nightingale in the words is Luther, but Wagner makes the music sound like Bach, and the vocal lines moving upward and downward along the scale remind me of John the Baptist, and the people of Nuremberg clearly intend the nightingale to represent Hans Sachs, and Hans Sachs himself probably thinks by now that the nightingale in the song is young Walther, and all of us who know the opera think at this point, 'Oh, the nightingale is surely Wagner.'" Such are the uses of metaphor.

A third pattern. All through the text there are references to shoes and boots, wax and pitch, leather and last. Young David clues us in to what all this means metaphorically: "Shoemaking and songmaking, I'm learning both together." In *Die Meistersinger,* shoes are a metaphor for songs. Sachs hammers away at Beckmesser's shoes whenever he finds a fault in his song. Eva comes to Sachs insisting that her shoes pinch, but what she really wants is not a well-made shoe but a well-made song for Walther to win the contest with, and while Sachs is busy working on the shoe, Walther appears in the doorway to sing the song. At the contest, Beckmesser, limping in his new shoes and unsure of his footing on the platform, attempts to fit the words of Walther's song to his own tune, with laughable results: neither the shoe nor the song fits.

These playful uses of metaphor have their deeper significances. With his ever-recurring references to baptism and songbirds and shoes, Wagner is suggesting a whole aesthetic. Art has, first, a kind of sacramental power in our lives. Art is also an extension of nature (music, especially, is an imitation of nature's sounds). And, practically speaking, art is the right way of making something, the *recta ratio factibilium.* Schopenhauer may have said the first, and Epicurus the second, and Aquinas the third. But none of them said it so imaginatively as does Wagner, in this opera.

Are you ready now to go deeper? John the Baptist, who presides over this opera, is a figure for Hans Sachs. This becomes clear in the first scene of Act III, when David sings: "On Jordan's bank stood John the Baptist . . . but here on the river Pegnitz, we call him Hans. Hans! Why, master,"—and he turns to Sachs—"today is your name day!" After that, the identification of Saint John with cobbler John really takes hold. Sachs ceremoniously christens Walther's newborn song, and the redemptive power of the baptized song goes to work instantly; it changes the lives of all five characters who sing the famous quintet. And eventually, on the riverbank in the last scene, it affects all of Nuremberg. We're sure by then that the saint is a figure for the shoemaker. But we might have known as much from the moment the curtain went up on Act I, from that all-important vesper hymn, when the people sing to the saint:

> Once our Savior came to thee,
> By thy hand baptized to be . . .
>   Baptist, teacher, Christ's first preacher,
>   Take us by the hand, there on Jordan's strand.

On the surface, this is conventional piety, appropriate to Reformation Germany. But in the overall context of the opera it works metaphorically, too. It is a prayer that Walther may come to Sachs and be baptized, and that Sachs may teach his people and raise them up, on a German strand, to a true appreciation of a new testament of song. So the prayer at the beginning of the opera is answered, metaphorically, at the opera's end.

If Sachs is John the Baptist, who, metaphorically, are the others? Their names will tell us. They are named for famous figures in the Bible who need redeeming. Like King David, and like Mary Magdalen, Wagner's David and Magdalene yearn for redemption—from a long apprenticeship, so they can marry at last. And like Eve, Wagner's Eva must be saved from Beckmesser, the devil of this piece, surely: his shoes are finished with pitch, not wax, and he exclaims "Zum Teufel!" ("Go to the devil!") at every turn.

Wagner doesn't press all this as far as he might have. He doesn't name his young hero Jesus. After all, we're in a shoe-making context, and the Bible's John said of Jesus, "The strap of *his* sandal I am not worthy to loose." And Wagner's young hero is hardly perfect; he sings wonderful songs, but he has a self-destructive streak, and he has much to learn. So Wagner associates his hero with that forerunner of Jesus, Adam. That's quite clear in Act II, when Walther and Eva plan to elope, and Sachs tries to stop them with a song, and Beckmesser too cobbles a song. What does Sachs sing?

When Adam and Eve fled from Paradise,
Lest they hurt their feet on the gravel outside,
God told an angel to make them shoes
Before the devil turned cobbler.

"What does that song mean?" Walther asks in the shadows. And Eva, who knows something about metaphor, says, "It's about us!" It is—if you think of Walther as Adam, Eva as Eve, Beckmesser as the devil, and Sachs as the angel barring the way in and out of Paradise, and if you're aware that, in this opera, shoes also mean songs.

The metaphorical levels reach their highest point, as is only fitting, in the words to the various drafts of the song that comes to our Adam in a dream. At first, the song is sacred in subject, drawn from the first pages of the Bible: a morning of wonderful light, a garden, a tree (the tree of life, in fact), a woman offering its fruit. Walther eventually says exactly what this signifies: Eve in the garden of Paradise—"Eva im Paradies."

Then the song becomes secular, about art: an evening when the urge to create is irresistible, a laurel tree (Apollo's tree, in fact), a woman peering through the branches. Walther eventually says exactly what this signifies: the Muse of Parnassus—"Die Muse des Parnass." The two first drafts of the song are about, respectively, religion and art, those co-metaphors in *Die Meistersinger.*

Poor, baffled Beckmesser, finding the first drafts, asks Sachs, "Is this a biblical song?" and the shoemaker replies, "You're missing a lot if you think just that!" He is right, of course; nothing in *Die Meistersinger* works on one level alone.

But when Walther conjures up more of his dream, his song does turn New Testament. The words call to mind medieval representations of the Virgin Mary, with stars in her hair and suns in her eyes, born in grace ("Huld-geboren"), chosen as in a Magnificat ("Ruhm-erkoren"). Wagner was eventually to say that the real inspiration for *Die Meistersinger* was seeing, in Venice, Titian's painting of the Assumption. That sounds very much like the *post factum* explanations he was accustomed to give of his work—but it does suggest that, by the time he came to realize that *Die Meistersinger* was going to be more than just a little comedy, he had begun to think his way through the biblical patterns in it.

In the Middle Ages they loved to sing how the "Ave" in *Ave Maria* was the reverse of "Eva." That is to say, how Mary, when she accepted the message of the angel, reversed the destructive process begun by Eve and began the whole process of redemption. The Middle Ages called Mary the new Eve, because through her came a redeeming from the flaw in human nature left by Original Sin.

Now we have come to the heart of *Die Meistersinger*. Now we can see why baptism is so important a symbol in it. Baptism saves us from Original Sin, and Walther's baptized song can save us from—well, what would it be in Wagner's scheme of things that, in traditional Christianity, is called Original Sin? Hans Sachs has the word for it: *Wahn,* that destructive streak, that mad streak that runs through human nature like some tragic flaw. Wagner, of all composers, knew it all too well. Sachs wonders about it over his books in Act III. He almost despairs over it. He hears it sounding in himself, like an echo out of his soul. Then, in a great moment, he rises from his books, walks to his window, and the realization comes to him, as morning light breaks over his city, that that basic human drive, *Wahn,* need not be destructive. The whole destruc-

tive potential in human nature can be reversed. Our *Wahn* can
be directed to creative ends. And that, for the rest of the opera,
is what Sachs proceeds to do.

As Wagner composed his greatest works, he came again and
again to the same profound realization: the flaw in our nature,
the irrational and potentially destructive force within us, can
also be powerfully creative, but it has to be directed. It has to
be, in the context of this opera, baptized. It has to be—to use
Wagner's own term, and the last word he ever set to music—
it has to be "redeemed." And the great value of art, which,
Sachs tells Walther, also arises out of that basic human drive,
is that it can meet that inner compulsion to destroy, and release
its potential to create. *Wahn,* like anything in human nature, is
potentially a beautiful thing, and art is its fairest flower.

Wagner called the house he built for himself Wahnfried:
peace from *Wahn,* or, better still, *Wahn* used for peace. He
knew that the force that propelled him was ambivalent. It was
terribly destructive. It defeated him, one way or another, all
his life. There was not one of his triumphs that was not somehow spoiled at the moment of triumph by his own self-de-
structiveness, his *Wahn.* In his person he was, to some degree,
the monster we often read about, plagued by *Wahn.* But in his
art, the same *Wahn* was powerfully creative. It produced from
within him a succession of mighty works in which he split
himself into Wotan and Alberich, Sachs and Beckmesser, Amfortas and Klingsor and all the others, and then proceeded to
drain away the evil, and bring together the good, and heal the
hurt, and understand, and find peace.

And so, if we listen, can we.

Wagner's critics are quick to object, "How could Wagner
sing about personal redemption and self-understanding when,
in his life, he never knew them?" But that, it seems to me, is
why he wrote opera after opera *about* them—out of the abun-

dance of his intuitive genius and the abyss of his personal need. As Hans Sachs puts it (metaphorically, of course), "A songbird sings because he has to. And because he has to, he can."

So, at the end of *Die Meistersinger,* there comes a great, cleansing baptism. Through the power of the song that came out of *Wahn* in a midsummer night's dream, the mastersingers of Nuremberg are freed from the bonds of convention. Young David is released from his long apprenticeship and given to his Magdalene. Walther learns to respect tradition and discipline his art. Eva, to Pogner's relief, is rescued from Beckmesser, who is exorcized (that is what happens to the devil at baptisms). And Sachs, who had almost despaired at human nature's flaw, does what in the opening hymn everyone prayed the Baptist would do: he teaches us about ourselves, and then takes us by the hand, there on Pegnitz's strand. The *Wahn* that infected all the characters on St. John's eve is washed away on the riverbank on Saint John's day. We in the audience rise from the long opera cleansed, baptized, purified. And the illuminated songbook that is *Die Meistersinger* turns its last shining page.

WHO IS
THE GRAIL?

Parsifal

I

In his essay "On Naive and Sentimental Poetry," Friedrich Schiller made a famous distinction between two kinds of artist. Perhaps in English we would call the two artists the objective and the subjective; in German Schiller called them the *naiv* and the *sentimentalisch*. It is a distinction we who love opera ought to know.

The *naiv* is an artist not conscious of himself as he works. He is at one with his art. He functions naturally within its traditions, and uses it for no ulterior purpose. He is objective and straightforward. His art is characterized by a deeply human quality, and has a directness, a profound simplicity that speaks immediately to all humankind. Who are the artists who are *naiv*? Homer first, and, in later literature, Chaucer and Cervantes and Shakespeare. Among painters I would cite Bruegel and Vermeer. And among composers, said Isaiah Berlin in another famous essay, there is Verdi.

The artist who is *sentimentalisch* is, on the other hand, not at peace with his art or himself. His work is taut with tensions. It often defies tradition and bursts out of the old forms. It *has* an ulterior purpose: to heal the tormented artist and his society and even, in some cases, the world itself. The artist who is *sentimentalisch* represents reality not objectively but with profound subjectivity. He looks inward, and cries out at what he sees. Who are the artists who are *sentimentalisch*? Virgil first, to set against Homer. And then, to cite only some of those influencing Wagner or influenced by him, Schopenhauer and Nietzsche, Baudelaire and Proust, painters both impressionist and expressionist, and, among composers, Richard Strauss and Giacomo Puccini. But the greatest of the *sentimentalisch,* as Schiller defined them, is unquestionably Richard Wagner.

Was there ever anarchist less at peace with himself, whose works so burst the bonds of convention, whose art is so permeated with insatiable longing? Was there ever a musician so preoccupied with ulterior purposes as this voracious reader, this compulsive talker, this dramatist drunk on ideas, this only composer to give his name to an "ism"? Was there ever an artist who looked so introspectively into himself? A full half century before Freud, Wagner's music dramas affirm, in thunder and wonder, the reality of what lies beneath human consciousness. His characters are the very archetypes Jung found there.

Isaiah Berlin said of Verdi that his "enormous popularity today . . . is a symptom of sanity in our time." It is good that we have Verdi's sanity, his humanity, in an era that seems to be characterized increasingly by irrationality and inhumanity. But because Wagner found those things, irrationality and inhumanity, in himself, and because he made eloquent works of art from what he found, it is a healthy symptom too that Wagner is more often performed and more carefully discussed and perhaps better understood today than at any time before.

Parsifal is about irrationality and inhumanity. It is also about the healing of those hurts. And its beautiful central symbol, the symbol of psychic healing and integration, is the Holy Grail.

What is the Grail? When he first appears in the opera that bears his name, Parsifal asks, "Who is the Grail?", indicating at the start how difficult it is even to ask the question that lies at the heart of this music drama.

The word *grail* seems originally to have designated not, as we might expect, a cup, or even, as etymology would indicate, a dish; early in the tradition the Grail seems to have been a kind of magic stone on which mysterious writing appeared and disappeared. Like the great stone slab that looms out of infinite space in Stanley Kubrick's *2001,* the Grail in the old legends was a means whereby an extraterrestrial intelligence communicated with mankind, as the cryptic writing on it came and went. In some traditions, the stone was said to produce food and drink magically for those who preserved it. The mere sight of the stone was sufficient to keep even the oldest attendant alive for seven days, and on its preservation the survival of the community was thought to depend. One long afternoon in the stacks of the Institute of Mediaeval Studies in Toronto, I satisfied myself that most scholarship on the subject sees the stone as originally the object of veneration in a pre-Christian fertility ritual.

But by at least the twelfth century, and very likely much earlier, the stone in the old legends was Christianized. Its powers were said to derive from a eucharistic host that, every year on Good Friday, a dove bore down from heaven and placed upon it. In the legends the stone became powerful beyond all telling because the sacramental food that appeared on its surface was the bread that was the Savior's body.

Meanwhile, quite different legends spoke of the Grail not as a stone but as a cup. Joseph of Arimathea, the disciple who (in

Scripture) arranged for Jesus' body to be buried in the tomb he had made for himself, also (in tradition) preserved the cup Jesus had used at the Last Supper. And when Jesus' side was pierced as he hung dead on the cross, Joseph was there with the cup to catch the blood that issued forth. The cup was lost, and for centuries across Europe tales were told about its turning up, now here, now there, powerful beyond all telling because it could still produce the wine that was the Savior's blood.

One legend dear to the hearts of Englishmen tells how Joseph brought the cup to Glastonbury, to the hill that later was to be associated with King Arthur, and buried it there—whence a stream of blood issued from the ground, while Joseph's staff, planted in the earth, became a blossoming thorn tree. Some years ago, at Glastonbury, I knelt at what Tennyson tells me are the tombs of Arthur and Guinevere, and I plucked a spray from what the local people told me is Joseph of Arimathea's thorn tree. But the stream of blood was not there for me to see, and the cup—no one could tell me where it is. What was true in the Middle Ages is still true today: we must find the Grail for ourselves, and not everyone is destined to find it.

Stone or cup, the Grail came to be sung of in tales all over Europe through the Middle Ages, when most people were devout Christians, did a lot of traveling (especially on pilgrimages), and venerated sacred objects (especially relics of the Passion of Christ). Anyone visiting the treasuries of European cathedrals today will find what are said to be pieces of the true cross everywhere from Spain to Turkey, often in reliquaries and chapels of astonishing beauty. Perhaps the most beautiful Gothic vaults and stained-glass windows in Paris, arguably in all Christendom, are in Sainte-Chapelle, which Saint Louis built, when he was king of France, to house the crown of thorns.

In those times as now, any baptized Christian could receive at Mass the sacrament of the Eucharist. In the great cathedrals of Canterbury or Cologne or Cordoba or Chartres, or in the little church on his own street, he could, if he fasted and did penance, receive the body and blood of Christ under the simple forms of bread and, in some eras, wine—the forms that Jesus had used at the Last Supper. But to medieval Christians, with their love of relics and their lively imaginations, the idea of receiving the sacrament from the very cup Jesus had used at that Supper, from the very cup that had caught his precious blood as he was lanced upon the cross—that idea was bound to take hold. And people thought, "Surely that ideal communion would be received only by the purest of the pure, after the greatest fasting and penance. Surely the Grail must be preserved somewhere, in some incredibly beautiful chapel that ordinary men could never find. And surely only the most perfect knights and heroes could ever drink from it."

As the Grail achieved mythic status, mythic ideas came to cluster around it: only one who does not seek the Grail will ever find it. The Grail itself calls those who will serve it. The man who is strengthened by the sight of it, and partakes of the nourishment it provides, is invincible in battle, and he battles only for good. Further, the man who is chosen and called by the Grail has to remain utterly chaste while he serves it, and so long as he is chaste a Grail knight can work miracles.

In our century, in T. H. White's Camelot book *The Once and Future King,* Lancelot, who has sinned with Guinevere, tells her and Arthur, when they are all grown older, how he was unable even to see the Grail when at last his expedition found it. Bravest and strongest he still was, but he was no longer chaste, and he could do no more miracles, and when he found the holiest of sights, he could not see it.

Wagnerians will by now have complained that, in all of this, I've spoken only of a stone that became a cup, and said nothing of a spear. But there is in fact nothing in Wagner's sources about the Grail's being a spear. What there is is the memory that Jesus' side was pierced by a spear, and tradition has preserved a name for the Roman soldier who wounded him—Longinus. A relic of that spear is still kept in the mightiest church in all the world, St. Peter's in Rome, where, near the high altar, Bernini fashioned a statue of Longinus, and Bramante built a balcony for the relic's veneration on Good Friday. But, sacred as that relic of the spear has been thought to be, it was never thought, through all the ages when the legend was developing, to be part of the Holy Grail.

And there is another spear in the legends, especially as they were told in Germany and France. A young king, Amfortas, who had custody of the cup, was wounded in battle by a spear, and the wound would not heal, and he kept the spear by his bedside. But that spear was not thought part of the Grail either.

It is important to mention these matters because here is where Wagner made his most significant change in the legendary materials. Working with Germanic versions of the Grail legend, he made the two spears one; his Amfortas is wounded by the very spear that had riven Christ's side. And then Wagner added that wounding spear to the cup as part of the Grail. In *Parsifal,* the Holy Grail is both cup and spear. And something terrible has happened to it: it has lost its power to strengthen and heal, for the cup has been reft of the spear, which evil forces have stolen away. And instead of writing on a stone, which the old legends would have provided, the voice of Jesus cries from the cup for the restoration of the spear.

It was a bold addition to the legend, and Wagner thought long and hard before he decided to make it. It is clearly intended to be significant, for it is presented to us in musical terms on the first page of the score. *Parsifal* opens with a hushed, long-spanned, all-but-unmeasured melody, which commentators call the theme of the Last Supper because it is shaped by the words Jesus used that night when he ate that supper with his apostles, and took bread and blessed it and said, "Take this my body," and then took the cup, filled with wine, and blessed it and said, "Take this my blood. And do this in memory of me." Those words, in the German version we eventually hear the Grail knights sing, actually suggest the outlines of Wagner's long opening theme:

"Neh-met hin mein _ Blut, neh-met hin mein-en Leib, __ _ auf dass ihr mein' _____ ge - denkt!"

After the strings have played that theme in unison, a high solo trumpet, surrounded by three oboes, repeats it over shimmering string arpeggios. That silver trumpet is, I think, the most beautiful instrumental touch in all of Wagner. At that moment, anyone who is searching for the Grail can catch a glimpse of it.

But eventually Wagner breaks his long melody into three parts, and uses the parts separately. This section indicates the cup:

and this thrusting fragment the spear:

while this expressive theme between them becomes the theme of suffering:

This is the suffering that comes on all of the characters in the drama because the cup is separated from the spear. So, in the opening phrase of the opera, when the motifs of cup and spear are separated by the motif of suffering, Wagner proclaims his revision of the old legends, and his symbolic insight into what the Grail stories might mean: there is suffering in the world because of the separation of what the cup and spear represent.

As if to put his amen to this, Wagner then has his brass intone a liturgical phrase that may be a kind of signature figure for him; it appears in four of his operas. Certainly he heard it many times in his young days in Dresden. It is the "Dresden Amen":

And then, as if to say, "I believe," Wagner adds the theme he himself called "Faith":

Wagner many be consciously evoking German Protestant tradition here; this theme is strongly reminiscent of a chorale by Hassler immortalized by Bach in the Saint Matthew Passion, "O Haupt voll Blut und Wunden" ("O Sacred Head Now

Wounded"). But Wagner immediately treats his Protestant theme as a Catholic celebrant might, stating it three times, each time in a higher key. That is the way solemn statements are made musically in Catholic ceremonies on Maundy Thursday, Good Friday, Holy Saturday, and Easter Sunday.

Perhaps it seems naive or sentimental to see Wagner's "Faith" motif as an expression of ecumenism. But Bach combined Protestant chorale with Catholic plainchant in the Credo of his B minor Mass, and Mozart did something similar in the fire-and-water scene in *The Magic Flute*. Wagner was aware of Bach's intention at least, and was not one to pass up an opportunity to do something like it, in a work that is very much about reconciliation.

But *Parsifal* is also, beneath its Christian surfaces, about many more things than Christianity. Opinions on it have always been widely divergent. Often the same person has changed his mind several times on it. The most famous of these is Friedrich Nietzsche, who first described *Parsifal* as an evil work, "an attempt to assassinate basic human ethics, an outrage on morality." Then Nietzsche found, when he read the *Parsifal* text, "poetry of the highest order" and, when he heard the *Parsifal* prelude, "a wisdom and perception that cuts through the soul like a knife." And then again, *Parsifal* became for him the work in which Wagner had forsaken his classic Greek ideals and sunk at the foot of the cross.

Anyone who knows *Parsifal* will know what Nietzsche meant by each of those remarks, and still find the disturbing, ambivalent work one of our great human testaments because, perhaps more in *Parsifal* than anywhere else, Wagner showed himself the artist Schiller defined as *sentimentalisch*—a word I would finally translate, in Schiller's sense, as "self-conscious" or, better still, "conscious of what lies within the self." In *Parsifal,* Wagner looked deeply into himself and, out of the dark and terrifying things he found there, wrote one last opera on one of mankind's most wondrous symbols, the Holy Grail, to heal the hurt he saw within, to reconcile and integrate. In his own symbolic terms, he went on a quest within himself to bring the spear back to the cup.

Wagner's works are as profound as Verdi's but utterly different. Schiller, who thought both the *naiv* and the *sentimentalisch* valid approaches to art, would have said that each of the two composers in his own way represents humanity, and that we need them both. And we are blessed to have them both.

I I

"Who is the Grail?" asks Wagner's young Parsifal in Act I, as old Gurnemanz puts his arm around him and takes him through a dark forest to the Grail's castle.

"If you are called," the wise man says, "that knowledge will come to you." Gurnemanz hopes that the boy is the "reine Tor," the innocent fool that the Grail knights believe will someday come to help them, that he will be "made wise through compassion" and will go questing for the lost spear, find it, and restore it to its rightful place with the cup they have reverently preserved.

Then, as the music moves wondrously forward, distant bells begin to toll, and the tall forest trees around the two figures change almost imperceptibly to the soaring vertical lines of a castle shaped like a Gothic cathedral. The boy exclaims that, though everything is changing around him, he himself hardly seems to be moving. And the wise old man explains, in one of Wagner's great lines, "You see, my son, time becomes space here."

Musically and dramatically this is a moment to leave the listener lost in awe. And it is important too for understanding this last work of Wagner's, a work in which we really do seem for long half hours to be passing through some changing but timeless space, wondering who and where and what we are.

There's an equally breathless moment in Act II. The innocent boy, who has not understood what he saw in that castle in the forest, now receives his first kiss from the mysterious woman, Kundry, who longs to do good but, in different incarnations through the centuries, has done only evil, and lured heroes to their deaths. Suddenly, with the dawning of sexual awareness within him, the boy is conscious of the human condition, of its potential for goodness and evil, of the profound flaw and hurt in it. He thinks back to what he saw but did not understand in that castle in the forest—the suffering Amfortas, who still preserves the Grail cup but has lost the spear, who has in fact been wounded by the spear with a wound that will not heal. Parsifal remembers how he felt the pain of Amfortas in his own soul. Now he knows that it was Kundry's kiss that brought Amfortas to his endless suffering. He also realizes now that the voice he heard issuing from the cup, "Rescue me from hands that are guilty," was the voice of Jesus himself calling to him, as if from within his soul, to bring the spear back to the cup.

Then, in Act III, Wagner, in one of his massive recapitulations, takes us back again to the castle of the Grail. Years have passed, and Parsifal has wandered across a wasteland, and it is Good Friday. As before, Parsifal hardly seems to move at all as he passes through the subtly changing landscape where time becomes space. This time, however, he approaches the castle not through a dark forest but through a radiant meadow. This time the wise old man does not lead, but follows, for now Parsifal has come not as an unknowing boy but as a man who knows the flaw, the hurt in the world. This time the ambivalent Kundry accompanies him, for Parsifal has turned the evil potential in her to good. This time the wounded Amfortas will be healed, for Parsifal carries aloft the long-lost spear with which he will make the Holy Grail, once more, complete and whole.

Parsifal enters the castle at the terrible moment when Amfortas exposes his bleeding wound and orders his knights to draw their swords and end his suffering. "Only one weapon can heal the hurt," Parsifal sings. He touches the spear-point to the wound. "Be purified," he proclaims, "whole and absolved. And blest be all your suffering, for it has made me wise. It has taught me compassion."

The bleeding stops. The whole enclosed space grows dark. Parsifal places the spear on the Grail stone, with the cup. The spear-point begins to glow, just as the cup always has at moments of unveiling. For a few moments, the only illumination is the light from the spear and the cup. The incredibly beautiful music that began the opera returns, more awe inspiring even than before because the themes of the cup and the spear are no longer separated by the theme of suffering.

Then a ray of white light breaks from the dome, and the dove that, in the old legends, renewed the Grail's power every Good Friday appears and hovers over Parsifal's head. As Parsifal raises the cup and traces a benediction in the air, Amfortas and Gurnemanz and the knights all kneel and open their arms upward to the light. Kundry sinks slowly to the ground—now, after all the centuries, released from her cycle of reincarnations. And innocent boys' voices, from the dome we cannot see, sing the phrase that, if any phrase does, contains the secret of understanding this mystifying music drama: "This is the greatest miracle of all. Redemption has come to the Redeemer."

And we might well ask, "What does it all mean?"

Partial answers can be provided on many levels. Because Wagner was, from the writing of the *Ring* onward, steeped in the works of his contemporary Arthur Schopenhauer, many commentators have seen *Parsifal* as a final testament to that philosopher's central ethical concept, *Mitleid*—empathy or compassion. The world's sufferings may be alleviated by acts of *Mitleid* done by selfless people who have seen so deeply into the human condition that they feel the sufferings of others in themselves. Wagner embodies Schopenhauer's concept in his hero, and proclaims it through the voice that rings through the Grail castle at the end of the first act: "Durch Mitleid wissend"—"Made wise through *Mitleid*."

Further, in line after line of the dialogue in *Parsifal,* the characters seem to feel the gravitational pull of what Schopenhauer called *Wille*—the force that, the philosopher said, animates all the world, and causes insatiable longings. So Amfortas says, "My wound breaks out again, renewed by the font of my longing." And Kundry shouts, "Yes, that is my curse—longing, longing." And Klingsor sings of his "untamed torment of longing." And Parsifal, after he has learned to feel in himself the sufferings of others, says, "The longing, the terrible longing that overcomes my senses." For Schopenhauer, *Wille* was the source of all human suffering, and he taught that we could find no peace until we denied it and overcame it. The initial step, he said, was a kind of personal chastity. A person's understanding of pain has to come first from within himself. When he sees his own pain as part of the pain of the whole world, he can at last open up to the world and, in *Mitleid,* actually come to feel the sufferings of others in himself. Made wise through compassion, he finds fulfillment in alleviating the sufferings of others.

Clearly, on one level at least, *Parsifal* is Schopenhauerian. But almost as many details in the text, and much of its ethical feeling, too, seem to reflect another of humankind's great teachings on suffering—Buddhism, which leads its believers away from their longing and pain toward a promise of Nirvana. And as a classicist listening to *Parsifal,* I think too of the

Greek tragic writer Aeschylus and the great moment in his *Agamemnon* when the chorus sings "Pathei mathos" ("Man learns though suffering"), almost a Greek translation of "Durch Mitleid wissend." While he was writing *Parsifal* Wagner was reading not only Schopenhauer but the classic Buddhist and Greek literatures as well, and he exclaimed that that chorus in the *Agamemnon* was the finest thing he had ever read.

Then there are other, less pleasant levels to *Parsifal*. A quarter of a century ago we were encouraged to see it as, among other things, an anti-Semitic tract, as an act of self-adoration, as the gospel of a new religion of art, a receptacle of all that was bad in nineteenth-century thinking. Some of that it may well be. Wagner always needed ideas to fuel his creative forces. Many of the ideas that came from his reading and from within himself were profound and compassionate. Some of them were, at best, dubious. Some of them were contemptible. Wagner was more and more dependent on the stimuli of ideas as he grew older, when his musical powers were still strong but the will to keep working began to flag. His letters and prose writings during his *Parsifal* period make for sorry reading, and we have to remind ourselves, reading them, that our greatest geniuses, especially the *sentimentalisch* among them, are often tormented, destructive, even self-destructive people. That is why they create. That is why their works are about healing.

So *Parsifal* is many things beneath its Christian surfaces. But because the overlay of symbols is Christian, it would be wrong not to see a Christian level in the work. In fact, most commentators in recent years have returned to the once-unfashionable view that *Parsifal* is quite specifically Christian, though not so simply as might at first appear. (Is anything simple in Wagner?)

Wagner's attitude toward Christianity was deeply ambivalent. He thought its founder a man of immense compassion, and its symbols resonant and beautiful. But he thought too that over the centuries Christians had buried Christ's message under a mass of irrelevant dogma. And in his own century Christianity seemed to have all but collapsed as a moral force. It had preserved the ceremonies but lost the purpose—if you will, preserved the cup but lost the spear—of its founder, whose voice cries out from the midst of its mysteries, "Redeem me, rescue me, from hands that are guilty."

Parsifal is, then, not so much Christian as it is *about* Christianity. About the healing of a wounded, suffering Christianity. In Wagner's words, "When religion becomes artificial, art has a duty to rescue it, by demonstrating that the mythical symbols which religion would have us believe literally true are only figurative, and by revealing, though idealized representations of those symbols, the profound truths they conceal." Like many before and after him, Wagner saw Christianity as the most beautiful of myths, a grand illusion that had power in its symbols to uplift and exalt. He turned to it when he saw his society caught up in an advancing wave of materialism. One of his last statements, before his death in Venice, was "If we cannot save the world from its curse, at least we can present it with symbols that will direct it to deep insight, and the possibility of saving itself."

All the same, though I am a professed Christian, and committed to ongoing reform in the church, it isn't Christianity I find most in *Parsifal*. It's world mythology. Hearing *Parsifal,* I always hear the myth of the hero—that figure known in a thousand different cultures, who passes from boyhood to manhood, from innocence to awareness, befriending his shadow side (Amfortas), defeating his destructive feminine (Kundry) to release its creative forces, confirmed in his mission by his wise old man (Gurnemanz), and reconciling all of these opposites within him around a central symbol that is his Self (the Grail).

That is the terminology of Carl Jung, and the hero myth as outlined in Joseph Campbell's book *The Hero with a Thousand Faces.* If it seems too clinical and academic a blueprint for Wagner's opera, we should remember that Wagner used myths for his subjects at a time when romantic Germans such as Feuerbach and Friedrich Schlegel and Herder were beginning to say what most mythologists say today—that man's myths are not idle stories but repositories of truths about himself.

So I can come in the end to the simplest of all explanations. *Parsifal,* with all its mysterious symbols and mystifying characters, is about me. About what happens within me, or you, or any of us who is human and flawed and suffering. The timeless, spaceless forest-castle we approach without even moving is our inner self, where there is hurt to be healed and need for reconciliation and integration and purpose and peace. The sufferings of Amfortas and Kundry are our own. Klingsor's self-destructive hatred we all feel. Parsifal's call to a chaste—that is, selfless—quest is our own vocation selflessly to heal ourselves. The integration, within the soul, of male and female principles symbolized by the spear and the cup is the miracle each of us is called to work within ourselves.

So the innocent boy led through the unconscious forest to the castle deep within it and not really distinct from it, that innocent boy asks not "What is the Grail?" but "Who is the Grail?" The Grail that calls out to be redeemed, rescued, restored to wholeness—that is your self, your soul, you. Your own integration is what you are questing for. The greatest miracle of all? Your own perfection. Redemption to the Redeemer? You can redeem yourself. Who is the Grail? You are the Grail.

That is what we can say of *Parsifal* from the perspective of Schiller, who distinguished between *naive und sentimentalische Dichtung,* between art that is unselfconscious and art that is, like Wagner's, profoundly conscious of the self, art that looks inward, doesn't shrink from what it sees, and attempts to drain away the evil and bring the good together. Wagner once said it was the purpose of art to make the unconscious conscious. *Parsifal* does that. It dramatizes what takes place, or can take place, within each one of us.

I hope that what I have said about *Parsifal* will help you understand it more, and wonder about it more. But in the last analysis it is not my but your response to its pleading that matters. Your healing, your wholeness, your questing, your onward struggle to become the person you have it in your soul to be.

Faust
Courtesy Winnie Klotz, Photographer
Metropolitan Opera Association Inc.

FRENCH OPERA

THE MATTER
OF MELODY

Faust

Gounod's *Faust* was once the most popular opera in the world.
Even now, at the Opéra in Paris, it is nearing the three-thou-
sand-performance mark, which may be a house record for any
opera ever presented anywhere. At Covent Garden it was
played every season from 1863 to 1911, and until World War
II it was a full hundred performances ahead of all the other
works in the repertory there. In Budapest it still tops the list
of performance totals, as it has in the city that spans the Dan-
ube for a full century. It opened the old Metropolitan on 39th
Street and Broadway, and it was done there so often that the
redoubtable critic of the *New York Times,* W. J. Henderson,
dubbed the Met not the *Festspielhaus* ("the festival house," as
at Bayreuth), but the *Faustspielhaus* ("the house where they
play *Faust*"). Italians took it early to their hearts, and it was in
Italian that our great-grandparents almost invariably heard it.
But the Germans discovered it first, after France had shown
little initial interest, and in Germany it was so often done in
repertory that it was renamed *Margarethe,* to distinguish it

from that national treasure Goethe's *Faust,* which was much more respected but also much less often performed.

Gounod's *Faust* is overwhelmingly important in the history of operatic singing. It is impossible even to think of such great voices of the past as Patti, Melba, Eames, Nordica, the de Reszkes, Plançon, Chaliapin, Caruso, di Stefano, and Bjoerling without thinking of *Faust.* That superb artist Marcel Journet sang Gounod's Méphistophélès more than a thousand times. No wonder, when I was a boy, the popular image of opera was of a devil in red tights.

I used to save my pennies then to buy excerpts from the great operas, in the sheet music section at Sears and Roebuck. And in every volume, there were more pieces from *Faust* than from any other opera. As a result, the tunes most often heard on our piano at home were invariably from *Faust.* I had to regard it as one of the great operas when, on the Metropolitan broadcasts, I heard it conducted superbly by Sir Thomas Beecham, and sung by the stylish likes of Pinza and Rethberg and Richard Crooks.

Style is all in Gounod's elegant writing. And if *Faust* is less popular today, one reason is that Gounod asks for a special quality—a subtlety, a Gallic sensitivity—that we seem to have lost in recent decades.

Then there is the matter of melody. Fifty years ago, Sigmund Spaeth used to say on the broadcasts that *Faust* could boast thirteen "number one" hit songs, while *Carmen* had only eight, and *Aida* seven. That was the great age of popular song in America, and melody—the air that, once heard, is never forgotten—was what we wanted on the *Hit Parade* and also what we wanted when, with only a few radio stations on the dial, we tuned in to hear the broadcasts from the Met. Today's listeners, with perhaps more sophistication, will do without melody if they can be gripped by a dramatic experience. And if *Faust* is not so popular as it once was, that is another one of the reasons. Reviewing the recent biographies of Caruso and Chaliapin in the *New Yorker,* Naomi Bliven remarks rightly that "popular music seems less tuneful today than it used to be; perhaps the earlier fading of operatic melody was prophetic." She continues, "We have been used to thinking of melody as an indestructible cultural creation, like romantic love, but perhaps melody is like monarchy—the product of a particular period in Western civilization." *Faust* seems to have lost its hold on the repertory here and around the world about the time popular music and much else changed, in the mid-fifties and sixties.

Now people have somehow accepted the uncritical notion that Gounod's *Faust* is a mere succession of old-fashioned tunes, and is hopelessly inadequate as drama. Today there is no lack of sophisticates who, when they think of Gounod's *Faust* at all, think of it with contempt. "It is," they say, "a bourgeois blasphemy against Goethe's *Faust.*"

Well, it goes without saying that Gounod is not so profound as Goethe. As Brahms said when his work was compared, unfavorably, with Beethoven's, "Any fool can see that!" Goethe's philosophical Faust is a figure based partly on his own life's experiences. (Goethe loved and left an innocent girl when he was a young student, and he felt the guilt of it for the rest of his days.) His Faust is also, like himself, a man who searches for meaning not just in romantic love but in all forms of human activity until, blind as Oedipus, he sees that the searching itself is the meaning he sought. He loses his soul to find it, saving himself by his relentless creative activity. All along, God has seen the good and the evil in Faust's nature, and permitted Mephistopheles to have his way with him so that the good could grow with the evil. Thus Satan unwittingly furthers the work of God in man. Goethe, in short, remythologizes Christianity, using its symbols to feel his way, over a period of some sixty years, through the great questions of life, art, and faith. His *Faust* is a hymn to the creative energy of God at work in man. We do not take its medieval symbols literally. It is a work of rationalism for a new romantic age but, like all classics, it speaks to all times and places.

Gounod's *Faust,* on the other hand, clings to the conventions of middle-class nineteenth-century Parisian piety. It asks us to take the old story literally, and that very few people can do today. It is not insignificant that Gounod's *Faust* reached its greatest popularity in the Victorian era. The part of Goethe it uses is, when divested of its prologue and reduced to a simple narrative, something of a Victorian morality play, in which carnal sin is punished. And it is the woman, not the man, who is made to suffer. That, certainly, is less acceptable today than it was in the day when the phantom of the opera carried Christine Daaé off to his lair during a performance of Gounod's *Faust,* the Victorian time when England's queen, in her last illness, asked to hear pieces from Gounod's *Faust,* and smiled whenever she recognized a familiar tune. Once again, *Faust* began to lose its hold on the repertory at about the time we called an end to the double standard in sexual morality.

Ought one then to compare the four hours' traffic on Gounod's stage with the hundreds of pages of Goethe's immense and virtually unstageable play? To some extent one may, because Gounod challenges comparisons with the whole of Goethe's *Faust,* and not just with the initial love story, when he introduces, late in the evening, a ballet with classical figures and, at the close, a resurrection chorus. Some recent scholarship indicates that part of that chorus and perhaps all of the ballet may not be by Gounod at all, which might absolve him of some of his failure to measure up to Goethe. But there have always been those who will point out that Gounod suffers even when his opera is set alongside the operatic *Faust*s of those three B's, Berlioz, Boito, and Busoni. And they have a point. Consider the way the three other versions end. Berlioz concludes with a ride to hell and an ascent to heaven that still present one of the supreme challenges in symphonic and choral literature. Boito ends with the windstorm of an omnipotent God driving Mefistofele to further unwitting execution of His will—at least that is the way Norman Treigle performed it so unforgettably. Busoni's Doktor Faust resurrects his dead child and, dying himself, breathes his own life into the body while a spoken epilogue proclaims, "Still unexhausted all the symbols wait." All three endings are dramatically compelling because they reach out to suggest something of the cosmic significances Goethe found in the old myth. Gounod's ending, by comparison, is an Easter chorus that is an embarrassment to conductors and stage directors alike and is often cut from twenty-six to twelve measures.

But we who love Gounod will hurry in to say that the soaring, climactic "Anges Purs" that precedes the final chorus, the trio in which the victimized Marguerite triumphs over her unfaithful lover and the forces of evil, is one of the most effective pieces ever written for the stage, that it can still pull an audience to its feet, as it always did in generations past; and that in Act II, the famous Garden Scene, listeners who, in this age of blatant cacophony, have never heard romance set to music, can hear a series of arias unparalleled for their grace and loveliness, and the most elegant love duet in all of opera.

Until Wagner wrote *Tristan,* the Garden Scene in *Faust* was thought the height of sensuous romanticism in opera; after Wagner, it may seem almost impossibly small-scaled. But *Faust* was originally conceived, and first performed, as an opéra comique—that is, as a small-scaled opera with spoken dialogue. Even when sung recitatives were added for Strasbourg and, ten years later, that unfortunate ballet was inserted to satisfy the demands of the Paris Opéra, *Faust* remained in essence what it was designed to be: comique, small-scaled, and bourgeois.

And that is the best way to view it today, for in terms of the genre it represents, *Faust* is a brave, forward-looking work. The full text of Barbier's libretto is only now coming to light, and it appears to have been a good deal more Goethian than it became after feverish Broadway-style revisions before opening night. Barbier and Gounod had to fight the directors of the Théâtre-Lyrique to keep their best ideas in the final version, and the usually calm Barbier stayed home the night of the premiere with nervous exhaustion. Gounod himself was just coming out of a breakdown.

So it was that *Faust* didn't get very favorable notices that opening night. Far from dismissing it as a mere succession of pretty tunes, audiences thought it daring and difficult and "German." Apart from the show-stopping "Soldier's Chorus" (a last-minute transfer from Gounod's unfinished opera *Ivan the Terrible*), its music was subtler and more learned than Parisians were prepared for. Few of Gounod's friends spoke to him after the premiere, and those who did advised him to modify his advanced style. Most of the press was hostile, and the work had to find its way slowly. Today, both Frenchmen and Germans seem to have forgotten that when the Lyrique temporarily folded, and the Opéra-Comique closed its doors to *Faust,* it was a triumphant reception in Germany that brought the work successfully back to France.

That first night, Berlioz, who had every reason to console himself that the new *Faust,* like his own several years before, was unappreciated by his fellow Parisians, generously pointed out the new opera's strengths: the opening measures with their fugal evocation of the old philosopher's despair, the first meeting of Faust and Marguerite on the street (was ever musical speech so delicately balanced between duet and recitative?), Faust's rapturous "Salut! demeure" and Marguerite's Gothic "Roi de Thulé," and, as the finest touch of all, the ecstatic moment at the end of the Garden Scene when Marguerite goes to her window:

Berlioz might have cited as well the poignant moment when a fragment of this recurs in the following act, pathetically twisted but still recognizable, as Marguerite, cursed by her brother, loses her mind:

I often test the worth of new books on opera by seeing what they have to say about *Faust*. A bad critic will dismiss it with, at best, a few condescending words. A good critic will acknowledge its astonishing melodic inventiveness, and realize as well that it is an indispensable opera, a cultural fact of considerable importance. That in France it refined, perhaps even redefined, the overblown Meyerbeerian concept of what opera should be. That it set a precedent for fitting music to the nuanced inflections of the French language. That, for the first time, it scaled French opera down at intimate moments to something resembling conversation. That with Marguerite, Gounod virtually created the species of soprano now known as lyric. That the shadows in Marguerite's garden have cast their languid influence across a century of French music; the stage works of Bizet, Saint-Saëns, Massenet, Delibes, and Lalo, not to mention some of the instrumental music of Franck, Fauré, and D'Indy, stand in those shadows. And have any of them really surpassed the sensuous quality of that moment at the beginning of Gounod's scene, when the strings, expectant and sinister, whisper like the wind through the leaves?

In the last analysis the case for *Faust* will always rest on its melodies, some of the most beautifully crafted, luminously scored melodies ever written, melodies that stay in the memory as good melodies should, and also delicately etch the characters, and, in the Garden Scene, lead the listener on inexorably to that moment at Marguerite's window—a superbly realized dramatic moment that, in its day, only a great critic appreciated, and only a master composer could have written.

UNANSWERED
QUESTIONS

Les Troyens

Deep in the vaults of the Vatican Library there rests a lordly, venerable manuscript called the Codex Palatinus. It is the oldest manuscript to contain virtually all of the writings of the poet Virgil, who lived out his lifetime in Italy just before the birth of Christ. Usually, with a Latin author from antiquity, we are lucky if we have a manuscript as close to him as the twelfth century. But with Virgil, the most quoted and loved of all ancient writers, manuscripts from the sixth and fifth and even the fourth centuries have survived. Florence and Verona and Sankt Gallen have some of them, but the others rightly reside in Rome, in the library of the popes. Rightly, for Virgil's greatest work, the *Aeneid,* is the epic of Rome, of its ambivalent past and its long future. It is also an epic of spiritual fatherhood, of the *pius Aeneas,* the faithful Aeneas. So it is fitting that the noblest copies of the poem rest in the library of the spiritual leader whom his people call father, who has sometimes been named Aeneas, and who has twelve times chosen for himself the name Pius. And it is fitting that the Codex

Palatinus lie in the heart of the city it proclaims will live forever.

One year I taught in Rome. In fact, I taught Virgil's *Aeneid* there, to young American students. And that year I realized my ambition to see the Codex Palatinus. Doing so was not exactly easy. I had to convince the serious librarians in the Vatican that I was, if not a serious scholar, serious at least about seeing the great Virgilian manuscript. The librarians were understandably wary of entrusting one of their deathless treasures to my mortal hands. They looked on me suspiciously as one who was in pursuit of an aesthetic experience, not a scholarly one. Well, they were right.

But in the end, they brought the fourth-century tome to my assigned desk, and carefully placed it on my assigned lectern. I was given detailed instructions, which I was careful to follow. My hands trembled as they touched, my eyes misted as they scanned, those ancient pages. The familiar Latin lines, in beautifully clear capital letters, looked out at me searchingly across the centuries.

Here first were Virgil's *Eclogues*: Titure, tu patulae. The words whispered and rustled and sang in their hexameters. These are the young Virgil's little pastoral poems, half set in a never-never land he called Arcadia, half set in the devastated Italy of his own day, a land torn apart by a century of war. The *Eclogues* are an invitation always to read Virgil as a metaphor. In them, the young poet wonders, "Will our world heal itself, or will it give way to the self-destructive forces within it?" Beneath their delicate surfaces, the ten Arcadian miniatures of shepherds and satyrs and swains dramatize a great moment in history, a time between war and peace. They all but predict the imminent birth of Christ. But we can never be sure of what they mean. They are elusive and subtle and sad. The promise of rebirth is there in Arcadia. Death is there too.

And here, before my eyes as the pages turn, are Virgil's *Georgics*: Quid faciat laetas segetes. Instructions on plowing, tending vines, breeding livestock, caring for bees. Love of the land. A belief that a providential power is alive in the world, a power that needs man to work its purposes. Virgil, now in his thirties, thinks he may have been too pessimistic before. Rebirth is a possibility. Civilization can survive the destructive impulses in man. World peace has been won, and Italy has begun to rework its countryside. But then, to end his *Georgics,* Virgil tells a story we opera lovers know well: how Orpheus descended to the world of the dead to bring back his Eurydice, and won her, and, through human frailty, lost her. The poet uses myth to wonder again about rebirth and survival, and he finds, again, mostly sad and ambivalent answers. (And here pages of the manuscript have, I see, fallen away across the centuries.)

Finally, before my eyes, there is the great *Aeneid*. The panoramic story of the Trojan hero Aeneas, who survives the fall of his city and leads his followers over the sea to Carthage and then to Italy, who descends to the world of the dead to glimpse his future, and then fights long, agonizing wars to win his peace. This longest and last of Virgil's works is the saddest and most ambivalent of all. No hero is so flawed, so failed as the *pius* Aeneas. No universe is so full of chaotic forces and senseless suffering as the world through which he moves. No century, until perhaps our own, was so much in need of absolving its personal and national guilt as the century in which Virgil was writing, a century of war. Aeneas is a figure for a man of that century, a man who took up arms and won peace for the world, but at a terrible cost, a man called Caesar Augustus. The *Aeneid* was written for him. "Arma virumque cano," it begins. The words are perhaps the most famous ever written in Europe. "Arms and the man I sing"—the warlike arms of the man who made half the map of Europe Latin, and half of the whole world Western, forever after.

And the song? There it is before my eyes: the *Aeneid.* T. S. Eliot declared it a song more civilizing than any that ever had been, ever would be, ever could be—because it pondered that ever after, including our century, and counted the cost. Eliot called the *Aeneid* "the classic of all Europe." Though it did not prevent Dachau and Dresden from happening, you could say it foresaw them and wept the world's tears, the *lacrimae rerum,* prophetically for them. It also knew, this song, that the tears it wept would always be *inanes*—insufficient.

Virgil's *Aeneid* shaped the poetry of Ovid and the prose of Tacitus. Augustus used it as his conscience, Hadrian to tell the future. One book of it moved Saint Augustine to tears, one line of it sent Savonarola into monastic orders. Some of it found its way for a while into the canon of sacred Scripture itself. For Dante, the author of the *Aeneid* was "maestro" and "autore," a guide through the past and the world beyond. Michelangelo, painting the Sistine Chapel, gave Virgil a parallel place with the Bible in telling of man's fatal flaw and his future promise. Siena and Florence shaped their histories, Milton and Tasso fashioned their epics under Virgil's influence. Young Bernini, helped by his father, sculpted Aeneas escaping from Troy with his father on his back. Young Berlioz, helped by his father, trembled with emotion when he read, in Latin, of Dido gazing upward, searching for the light before she dies, and finding it.

All his life Berlioz was haunted by the *Aeneid,* and near the end of it he wrote, as an act of homage, *Les Troyens.* Not all of the *Aeneid,* just incidents chosen from little more than three books of Virgil's twelve. Not much at all of Virgil's searching for answers, of his theological sense of history, of his majestic "sadness at the doubtful doom of humankind." *Les Troyens* is mostly juxtaposed surfaces and contrasts, grand themes and noble, stylized feeling. In the tradition of the French lyric theater Berlioz provides a series of *tableaux vivants*. The long speeches in his opera seem to me a little chiseled and cold, classicism in the wrong sense. But most of *Les Troyens* is quick and tense with feeling, as a real classic must be. Gradually we are coming to see it as *the* classic of French opera. A lesser composer would have equipped his Trojans, destined out of defeat to found the greatest city in history, with an unequivocal, rousing theme, like the one Gounod gave his soldiers in *Faust,* or Meyerbeer his Huguenots, or Saint-Saëns his Israelites. But Berlioz's Trojans are unique. They are tough warriors from an exotic, fallen city, charged with a civilizing mission they do not fully understand. They are grandly barbaric, like wolves, and thick-tongued trumpets indicate their ambivalent sense of history:

Berlioz, named for Hector, the greatest Trojan of them all, caught something of Hector's Asiatic spirit in that remarkable march with its swirling triplets. Surely he had the sound of Virgil in his head when he wrote it. Virgil's meter is fashioned from a kind of triplet, the dactyl. Three syllables—a long followed by two shorts, as in the names Jupiter, Romulus, Hannibal. The dactylic hexameter is a rhythm that in Virgil's hands can be made to sound barbaric and quick, as when the Trojan cavalry thunders across the dusty plain:

quadrupedante putrem sonitu quatit ungula campum.

It can also suggest processional grandeur, as when Virgil says:

tu regere imperio populos, Romane, memento.

That line means, "Remember, O Roman, it will be your mission to rule the world." When Berlioz first parades his royal Romans-to-be, the Trojans, across his stage, the music is truly Virgilian. It suggested to one critic "the warriors who march in angular profile across some ancient sculpted frieze." True enough, but as Berlioz has his Trojans sing at that moment, "Attendez les accents!"—that is to say, "Listen to the rhythms!":

That's not just sculpture. That's meter. That thrusting music will fit the prophetic line "Tu regere imperio populos . . ." Its rhythm will fit the very first line of the *Aeneid,* a line you may still have by heart from your high school Latin class: "Arma virumque cano Troiae qui primus ab oris." "Arms and the man I sing. Troy's shores he once left forever."

Dactylic hexameters can also, in Virgil's hands, be made to sound as light and whispery as the darkness he made visible. In Virgil, sleep comes lightly, gliding down from the silent stars:

cum levis aetheriis delapsus somnus ab astris.

Berlioz conjures up the sound of that line in "Nuit d'ivresse," his whispering nocturne, his sleepy moonlit seascape, his love duet for Dido and Aeneas. In the words of "Nuit d'ivresse" he borrows from Shakespeare, turning English to French. But he was only following his master: Virgil, when he wrote his *Aeneid,* turned parts of Homer and Greek tragedy and Greek philosophy into Latin, because he wanted his poem to be, among other things, a compendium of the wisdom of the past. Berlioz introduces, for his moon-washed moment, that moment from the last act of *The Merchant of Venice* where Lorenzo says to Jessica, "The moon shines bright . . . In such a night / Stood Dido with a willow in her hand / Upon the wild sea banks, and waft her love / To come again to Carthage." The English "in such a night" becomes the French "par une telle nuit," and Berlioz accents his ⁶⁄₈ time so that Shakespeare in French comes out sounding like Virgil's hexameter:

Berlioz knew that he could not put all of the *Aeneid* on the stage. Even at the prodigious length he opted for, he had to sacrifice Virgil's greatest book, the sixth, the hero's descent to the world of the dead, passing through the darkness with a gleaming golden bough. Berlioz also had to sacrifice all the wars in Italy and the characters he loved most after Dido: Camilla, the Italian Joan of Arc, and Turnus, the Italian Lancelot. But he used what he could. Some things from the end of the *Aeneid* he knew he had to use. He took from there the poignant words Aeneas speaks to his little son, as he kisses him through the visor of his helmet and leaves for war: "Learn from me, my son, what it is to be a man and to suffer. Learn from others what it is to be happy."

Berlioz also knew he had to use Virgil's young poems, the *Eclogues* and the *Georgics*. He wrote echoes of both into the song his Iopas sings at Dido's court: "O golden Ceres, you bless the fields and bring happiness abounding to the young shepherd and the old farmer." And he achieved his subtlest combination of literary and musical effects in the offstage song of a character of his own invention, a young sailor singing high in the mast as his Trojan ship lies at anchor. The boy wonders whether he will ever sing again beneath the great trees of his Trojan mountain, where he bade his mother good-bye. He calls on the sea to be his mother now, and rock him on her breast. His sea song becomes a cradle song:

When Berlioz wrote that song, his own son was away from home, serving in the French merchant navy. "I thought of you, dear Louis, when I wrote it," he said in a letter. But the song is more than just a personal touch. It is truly Virgilian—prophetic and pessimistic. Berlioz has two plain-spoken soldiers hear it:

"He's dreaming of his homeland," says one.

"Which he'll never see again," says the other.

Then, under the song, the orchestra surges ominously, like the sea. The young sailor falls asleep. We never hear of him again. But those who know Berlioz's way with his orchestra suspect that this young sailor will be drowned at sea. And those who know Virgil are sure of it, for Berlioz has named the boy Hylas. And Hylas is the name of a mythical boy drowned in both the *Eclogues* and the *Georgics*.

Another sailor drowns famously in the *Aeneid*. He falls asleep at his post. A god sends him a dream, and when it comes gliding down to him from the silent stars,

cum levis aetheriis delapsus somnus ab astris,

he too drops to his death in the sea. In Virgil, the young and the innocent die. Virgil does not know why that must be, except that there are always wars. That is the way the world turns. Virgil wonders and weeps over that world.

And as Virgil's pages turn, I come to the end, in the Vatican Library, of his twenty-centuries-old poem. Aeneas stands on the last page, caught agonizingly in the act of killing so that civilization can survive. He has been assured that this is the will of God. But is it? The *Aeneid* ends ambivalently, abruptly, shockingly. Its words stare out at me now across a hundred generations of men. Virgil's unanswered questions crowd in on me. What is God? Why is there evil in the world? Why, in order that good may come, must the innocent suffer? What is the fatal flaw in man that makes him destroy? If we are so given to violence, what can the future hold for us? Will our world survive, or will we destroy ourselves?

Those are of course contemporary questions. But they were posed twenty centuries ago. Something of them is in *Les Troyens,* which the Metropolitan chose, most fittingly, to open its second century. As we face the future, Virgil's unanswered questions are questions we all must ponder.

SIX
CHARACTERS
IN SEARCH
OF A POET

_____

Les Contes d'Hoffmann

Where does an imaginative artist find his ideas? What made Kafka and Poe think up their weird, wonderful stories? Whatever possessed Hieronymus Bosch when he painted his grotesque canvasses? What demon lurked in the imaginations of Murnau and Wiene when they gave us their films *Nosferatu* and *The Cabinet of Dr. Caligari*? How, in Offenbach's opera, does the poet Hoffmann think up his three tales, each more marvelous than the last?

Maybe, in Luther's Tavern, it's the smoke rising from the meerschaum pipes that inspires Hoffmann. Or the beer bubbles singing in the kegs, or the wine in his glass, which he empties and fills over and over again. Maybe it's the boy Nicklausse, who never leaves his side. Or maybe it's that three of the students, clamoring for tales, are having bad luck with their girls. One says he loves a cold-hearted doll, another is snared by a brazen courtesan, a third dotes on a virtuoso artist. Hoffmann obliges all three by casting himself in their predicaments and spinning their suggestions into stories.

What seems most to inspire the stories is that Hoffmann is always unlucky in love himself. It is really his own predicament in Luther's Tavern that is refracted into the three distorting mirrors that are his three stories. Hoffmann is in love with the beautiful Stella, and she has finally agreed to see him that night when she is finished singing in the opera house next door. But her servant Andrès has sold her letter of assignation and the key to her room to another—to the sinister Councillor Lindorf. And Lindorf is listening in the shadows as Hoffmann tells his tales.

That is the situation that is elaborated in the tales Hoffmann tells. Each tale has six characters—in effect the same six characters who figure in the situation in the tavern. Hoffmann himself is the protagonist in each story, with the boy Nicklausse at his side. But in each story we also meet Stella the beautiful woman, and Lindorf the evil genius, and Luther the bumbling proprietor, and Andrès the jack-in-the-box servant. Only the names are changed.

First, Stella. She becomes in turn a doll, a courtesan, and an artist. Three different grotesques, but all somehow the same elusive figure. As his imagination takes wing, Hoffmann endows each lovely lady with some birdlike quality. The mechanical doll Olympia is like one of the songbirds in her song, "Les oiseaux dans la charmille." The courtesan Giulietta is called, by the evil genius who uses her, *l'alouette,* the lark. And the artistic Antonia sings of herself when she sings about *la tourterelle,* the turtle dove, vulnerable but ever true. Together the three ladies form a composite picture of Stella, singing next door in Mozart's *Don Giovanni* while the tales are being told.

Singing which role, we wonder? There are, after all, *three* ladies in *Don Giovanni*. Is Stella playing the soubrette Zerlina? Or the avenging Donna Anna? Or Elvira, slightly mad but ever true? There is so much for the operagoer to wonder at as

Hoffmann's stories begin to refract the situation in the tavern. Next, Lindorf. The three stories transform this mysterious figure (whom Hoffmann calls a "oiseau de malheur," a bird of ill omen) into three villains bent on destroying the poet: Coppélius, Dappertutto, and Dr. Miracle. Each of these figures is at one time or another called Satan, which ought not to surprise us, for the Lindorf who inspires them styles himself "a lover with a Satanic streak." One of Hoffmann's first lines is "The devil take me if I ever fall in love," and that of course is what happens, three times over, in the tales. Accordingly, Offenbach equips all four devils with the same tail-lashing motif:

Why is Hoffmann too blind to take effective action against the demons in his stories? Perhaps because all three opponents specialize in optical illusions: Coppélius (whose name is from the Italian for "eye socket") makes mechanical eyes and magic eyeglasses; Dappertutto (whose name implies that he sees through everything) collects shadows and reflections in mirrors; Dr. Miracle (whose name suggests he can suspend the natural order) treats an invisible patient and brings a picture to life.

The more we superimpose the three tales of Hoffmann one on another, the more correspondences we see. Andrès, the practically inarticulate servant in the tavern, reappears in the tales as the stammering assistant Cochenille, the monosyllabic hunchback Pitichinaccio, and the half-deaf butler Frantz. And Luther the hapless tavernkeeper, whose wife and wine are the object of so many student jests, is transmogrified in the tales into the hapless Spalanzani, losing a mechanical daughter;

Crespel, losing a real daughter; and Schlémil, losing his mistress and his life.

Are we being too ingenious? Is all this too complex for a libretto by Jules Barbier and Michel Carré, those authors so often maligned for tailoring the mighty texts of Goethe and Shakespeare to suit the sentimental demands of Gounod and Thomas? Well, their *Contes d'Hoffmann* was originally conceived not as a libretto, with music to cover over weaknesses, but as a spoken play, to stand or fall on its own merits. In fact, it was staged some thirty years before Offenbach set it to music. It was fashioned of course from the works of the real-life storyteller, the famous E. T. A. Hoffmann. But the libretto makes clever changes in the tales it uses. It makes Hoffmann the protagonist in each. It adds Dr. Miracle so that Antonia's story will have a satanic villain to match the one in Olympia's and the one in Giulietta's. It introduces characters from other tales—Cochenille, Pitichinaccio, and Frantz—so that even the bit parts in the three stories will correspond. And it eliminates features of the original tales—the spectacular suicide of Olympia's lover, the sinister doings of Antonia's father—because these would not align with their new concept. Barbier and Carré have been censured for softening the horror of the originals, but surely they had something else in mind: they wanted to show how an imaginative artist gets his ideas out of his own experience, and how those ideas shape themselves into revealing patterns.

But the canniest stroke of Barbier and Carré was to frame their three stories with details from E. T. A. Hoffmann's most psychobiographical tale, the one he called "Don Juan." A traveler wakes in the night to find that his hotel bedroom connects with a private box in an opera house. He wanders into the box. They are doing *Don Giovanni* below. As he watches, he hears a stirring behind him, and turns to see Donna Anna standing there. A kind of telepathic communication passes between them. They kiss. She makes him think that he is Don Juan or—is it all a dream?—maybe he is Mozart. In the morning the traveler wakes, in his bed, and learns that in the night past they really were doing *Don Giovanni* in the opera house next door, and that the soprano who sang Donna Anna died, mysteriously, in the night.

The man who told that tale, the real-life E. T. A Hoffmann, adored *Don Giovanni*. To have composed it, he said, would have been the joy of his life. In homage to the man who did compose it, he changed his third name to Amadeus. Now, think of that working in the three stories in Offenbach. The opera's Hoffmann stumbles through the stories like a reverse image of Don Giovanni. He equips himself with a companion Leporello (who even sings a snatch of Leporello's music). He pursues a Zerlina, an Anna, and an Elvira, and in each tale he has to deal with an ineffectual Ottavio and a stammering Masetto as well. And a supernatural Commendatore always gets him in the end. What a remarkable libretto this is!

It's small wonder that this libretto appealed to Jacques Offenbach, because he too loved *Don Giovanni*. He was proud when Rossini called him "the Mozart of the Champs Elysées" (and was no doubt stung when Wagner qualified that with a critical "He *could* have been a Mozart"). Popular as he was with operetta, Offenbach desperately wanted, in his last years, to succeed with an opera. But he was dejected and dying, racing against time, as he wrote this one work that could qualify for the title, and he left it incomplete. *Les Contes d'Hoffmann* survives in a bewildering mass of different editions, with bits here and there by other hands—a not inappropriate end to a work that had Amadeus Mozart spooking around beneath the surface.

But more and more of the original opera is now coming to light, and gradually we are discovering that the real resonance in this resonating work was added not by the librettists but by the composer—when he wrote the part of Nicklausse for female voice. Such trouser roles are of course a convention in opera. In French opera alone we have familiar examples in Siebel, Stephano, Frédéric, Jean, Yniold, Urbain, and Ascagne. But Nicklausse is more complex than any of these. Is he flesh or fantasy? He seems real enough in the real world of the tavern, in the opera's prologue and epilogue. But in the three tales he is curiously ignored by everyone except Hoffmann himself. He seems hardly to exist except as some projection of Hoffmann—some other side of him. In the tales, Nicklausse has the perspicacity, the wit, the instinct for survival that the blinded, self-destructive Hoffmann utterly lacks. In the Olympia act, he sees that Hoffmann is in love with an illusion; in the Giulietta act, he provides the means for Hoffmann to escape from the police; in the Antonia act, when Crespel draws a knife, he saves Hoffmann from death itself. So we are astonished when, after the tales are told, Nicklausse seems to *betray* his Hoffmann, and gives Stella away to Lindorf.

What is this Nicklausse? Is he Hoffmann's lover, and is this the explanation of the poet's curiously unsuccessful relationships with women? Or is he Hoffmann's Jungian anima, the feminine principle within the man, the source of his creativity but a potential threat to his psychological development? Or is he Hoffmann's muse, urging him into the pathetic situation in the tavern, prompting him to elaborate it in the three tales, and then denying him the personal fulfillment that would still his creative instinct?

Recent productions of the opera have restored the ending (and some, the beginning) in which Nicklausse actually appears as Hoffmann's muse. He sings, "And I, your faithful friend, whose hand has dried your eyes, I who sent your sorrows wafting upwards in dreams . . . am I nothing? I love you Hoffmann! Be mine!" Lover, anima, inspiring muse—Nicklausse may be all of these. But the considerations are possible only because Offenbach wrote the role for a woman to sing.

If this is Offenbach's luckiest stroke, there are still a hundred other felicitous touches he added with his music: the marvelously evocative student choruses, the curious mechanical minuet at Spalanzani's, the electrifying moment when the Venetian characters begin to speak, and kill, over the rocking, mocking strains of the "Barcarolle," the poignant lyricism of Antonia's duet with Hoffmann, and above all the tension of the trio when Antonia's dead mother comes alive in the picture on the wall.

It comes as something of a shock to discover that Offenbach originally wrote the suspenseful music of that trio not for the appearance of the ghost of Antonia's mother but for an operetta called *Fantasio*. And that his sinister theme for Dr. Miracle in that scene was first heard twenty years earlier in a ballet called *Le Papillon*. And that Dappertutto's "Diamond Aria" was fashioned, by an unknown hand, from an overture Offenbach wrote for a piece called "A Journey on the Moon," for Monte Carlo. And that another unknown hand wrote the big ensemble in the Venice act, the famous Septet. Like the "Diamond Aria," the Septet became part of the opera only after some imaginative reconstruction in Berlin in 1905. It comes as still more of a shock to discover that the part of Hoffmann was originally written for baritone, and all four female roles for lyric soprano. And that the proposed order of scenes was not at first Olympia, Giulietta, Antonia—as we usually have it today—but that Giulietta's scene was intended to come last, and she was to die at the end of it, as the other ladies do. Most astonishing of all is the fact that the best-known number in the score, the "Barcarolle," was first composed to conjure up not Venice's canals but the depths of the Rhine; Offenbach first penned it for a failed opera called *Die Rheinnixen*.

All of this, and much more, is true. In his race against time, a race he eventually lost, Offenbach borrowed extensively from previous work, leaving the act he hoped would be his masterpiece, the Venice act, in so many versions that it was cut completely in the first run of performances. Some of *Hoffmann* was finished after Offenbach's death by the man from New Orleans who wrote the recitatives for *Carmen*—Ernst Guiraud. And the day after the German premiere, Guiraud's original scores were lost to a fire in Vienna's Ringtheater. Five years later a second fire, the terrible fire at the Opéra-Comique on May 26, 1887, destroyed much of the Paris materials. It is almost as if, like Hoffmann in the opera—or like the dying Amadeus Mozart—Offenbach, attempting greatness in his last days, was beset by some evil genius. Small wonder that, at Offenbach's funeral, the organist used bits of *Hoffmann* for the *Dies Irae* and the *Agnus Dei*.

Since then, the original publisher, Choudens, has issued a series of editions with different materials and alternate endings. The opera seemed to many critics only an interesting collection of set pieces until Hans Gregor at Berlin's Kurfürsten Oper in 1905 (like Walter Felsenstein at East Berlin's Komische Oper in 1958) went back to the original play for continuity and adapted Offenbach's music for his own ingenious purposes. And anyone my age will recall how, in 1951, the opera came alive when Sir Thomas Beecham and that famous movie partnership, Powell and Pressburger, reimagined it, perhaps too grotesquely, on the technicolor screen.

The gradual emergence of more and more of the original *Hoffmann* in recent years is something of a detective story with the last chapter still missing. A remarkable discovery was made about a decade ago by the conductor Antonio de Almeida, who is at present cataloguing the chaos in the Offenbach canon, as Köchel once did for Mozart. (Musicologists who refer to *The Marriage of Figaro* as K. 492 may soon be citing *Les Contes d'Hoffmann* as A. 554.) Almeida was searching through a collection of Offenbachiana in a villa near Paris and found a black folder that contained hundreds of pages of the opera in piano-vocal parts. It was an early version of the score as Offenbach had performed it one day at the piano, with the assistance of his four daughters and some friends, for two rival producers who were interested in staging the piece. Almeida communicated these pages to Fritz Oeser, who was then preparing what was hoped would be the opera's definitive edition. These and other recent findings have pretty well confirmed what we suspected from the first about Nicklausse: that he was intended by the composer and librettists to be an embodiment of Hoffmann's muse. The new discoveries also provide the boy with additional music to sing in each act. In fact, when the Oeser edition was first performed, at Cologne in 1980, Nicklausse had the second-longest role in the opera.

But in many ways Oeser has proved just as controversial with his new *Hoffmann* as he was with his *Carmen* two decades before. Opera houses hesitate to restore music Offenbach himself may have decided to cut, or to include music that Oeser himself presumed to write.

In the future, anything can happen. Recently in Paris a libretto turned up with a wholly new ending for the Venice act; in Salzburg, James Levine readied a new *Hoffmann* to mark the Offenbach centenary; and in Washington Michael Kaye prepared an edition based on 350 pages of previously unpublished autograph manuscripts, not mere piano-vocal parts but fully orchestrated.

The *Hoffmann* we know in the future may have much more dialogue spoken over music. The Olympia act will have a new trio and the Giulietta act a new gambling scene. And the opera will end not with Hoffmann alone in Luther's Tavern but with our six characters and the chorus singing an ensemble that comments on the opera's meaning.

But even when the last bit of scholarship has been expended on *Les Contes d'Hoffmann,* we shall still have to say that fate has, with an ironic taste for symbolism, left Offenbach's masterpiece in bits and pieces, like Olympia. Editors will continue to find that the opera ultimately eludes them, like Giulietta. But audiences will insist that, frail as it is, *Hoffmann* is an opera that really sings, like Antonia. It is a wonderful piece that reflects six characters in the spirit of Pirandello, and conjures up associations of the other side of Dr. Jekyll, and of Dr. Mabuse, Dr. Frankenstein, and Dr. Caligari. In one transformation or another it has held the stage for over a hundred years.

The reason for this is, I think, not hard to find. We are all of us fascinated with the imagination, how it works, and what it can do. And Offenbach and his librettists have, for once, really shown how the figures of a creative artist emerge out of the imagination—in this case, out of the Mozart-loving, Doppelgänger imagination of that master teller of tales, E. T. Amadeus Hoffmann himself.

PHRASES
MASSENÉTIQUES

Manon

Jules Massenet came to me in a dream one night, looking down from the stars. I seemed for a moment to hear the elegant, whispery music he wrote for Des Grieux's dream in the second act of *Manon*.

"So you're going to tell the radio audience about Manon," he said. "You're going to tell them all about one of my beautiful women who went wrong. Well, be sure you tell them about the notebook."

"The notebook!" I exclaimed as I clutched my pillow. "Of course. That's where I'll start."

It was a beautiful woman, Massenet's mother, who presented him with his first little boy's notebook, and this commandment: "If during the day you have said or done anything wrong, you must confess it in writing in these pages. Perhaps that will make you hesitate before doing anything wrong again."

Little Jules, youngest of his father's twenty-one children, began by bravely recording a theft of chocolate squares. And

169

he found it was delicious, more delicious than the chocolate, this confessing the wrong things he had done, for Mother would invariably be pleased with his courage, and give him a warm, forgiving embrace. Massenet tells us all this in the modestly immodest volume that the notebook grew into, *Mes Souvenirs,* and he adds, "It wasn't long before I was munching on other and better chocolate."

There is hardly a hint in Massenet's *Souvenirs* of the poverty of his youth and the compulsive ambition that drove him to write nearly thirty operas and much other music. To hear him speak of it, composing seemed not much more than the effortless recording in a notebook of the confessions of beautiful women who hesitated only slightly before doing wrong.

Perhaps the essence of Massenet's art, and of how it draws delicately from life, is best seen in the aria Manon sings in the second act. She knows that, in a few minutes, her Des Grieux is going to be taken from her, and their poor but happy life on the Rue Vivienne will be over, and she will be off on a courtesan's career. She hesitates only slightly, trembling on the brink. She says good-bye, not to Des Grieux (how could she face him?) but to their little dinner table. Her "Adieu" must be the shortest and simplest aria in all of opera—just twenty-four measures long, only a fraction of the length of a popular song. Under the vocal line the orchestra provides only a succession of chords. But what wonderfully poignant chords they are! Ravel did not hesitate to use them, and with good reason. They are as eloquent as the chords in a Chopin prelude and, just by themselves, they shape a little drama. "It's hard to believe how tiny you are," Manon says to the inanimate thing, all but bringing it to life. And we think that the little table she says farewell to is very like the innocence she soon will lose.

It was at a luncheon table that Massenet, if we can believe his memoirs, first found the words to "Adieu, notre petite table." Writing *Manon,* he says, was as natural as eating or drinking. He merely dropped a hint to the most famous librettist of the day, Henri Meilhac, and within twenty-four hours was sent in return an invitation to lunch at Vachette's. And on the table he found, beneath his napkin, the first two acts of the libretto. The rest, he assures us, followed in just a few days.

Then he spent a quiet summer in The Hague, composing in the very room where the author of the original novel, the Abbé Prévost, had once lived. He would doze off in the Abbé's bed. "It was a great cradle," he records, "shaped like a gondola." After that, he'd rise to stroll, for inspiration's sake, through the dunes of the North Sea or the woods of the royal palace. "And there," he continues characteristically, "I made exquisite friends of the little deer who brought me the fresh breath of their muzzles."

After that, still in a kind of Disneyesque dreamland, there was the young girl selling violets for a couple of sous on the Boulevard des Capucines. "Her looks obsessed me," writes Massenet. "Her memory haunted me." He never spoke to the girl but kept her face in his mind's eye all the time he wrote. She *was* his Manon—so much so that when his work was done, he saw to it that she was given a pass for the whole run of performances that first season.

All of this, whether true or less than true, is instructive, especially for those who come to *Manon* after the full-throated passions of Puccini's opera on the same subject. Not for Massenet the unabashed, extraverted ways of Italy. A Frenchman, he understates. His *Manon* is nothing if not subtle. In every detail he gives us about writing it—the napkin on the table, the bed like a rocking cradle, the soft-muzzled deer, the anonymous flower girl—there is a combination of opposites: a spontaneity that is studied, a laziness that is insistent, a preoccupation with sexuality that is almost innocent. And that is what the opera he wrote is like: carefully observed, tender, sensuous, and, above all, subtle.

Romain Rolland spoke, though not altogether approvingly, of "the Massenet that slumbers at the heart of every Frenchman." I'm not a Frenchman, so I won't comment on that statement, but I will say that anyone who has heard *Manon* and has also been to France will say that *Manon* is something like Paris. If the hurried tourist is not charmed, Paris does not care. And Massenet? He'll make a slight effort to please, but not to overwhelm. That he left to Puccini, who soon took up the challenge. Massenet knew that his own strength lay in his unique gift for understatement.

The libretto put together for Massenet from Prévost's novel is a remarkable piece of work. It condenses the original into six scenes, each of them set in a different locale to give some idea of the novel's sweep and variety. Puccini's later version is actually more faithful to Prévost in plot details; Massenet had to make Prévost's sordid, cautionary tale conform to the comfortable bourgeois tastes of the Opéra-Comique. So his Manon is not promiscuous, as in the original, nor does she die ignominiously in exile in the New World. His Des Grieux does not turn thief and murderer. (In the novel, where Des Grieux tells the story and remains the psychological center, he disintegrates completely.) Similarly, Massenet's Lescaut is changed; he becomes Manon's cousin, not her brother; a scapegrace but not, as in the novel, a pander. And the sinister Guillot of the novel is made a figure of fun in the opera. With all this rearrangement, Massenet's piece becomes essentially the story of two innocents too much in love and spiraling downward.

Massenet made many suggestions about the libretto, and is largely responsible for the inclusion of the scenes at Saint-Sulpice and the Hôtel de Transylvanie. And in writing the music, he made, I should say, three contributions to French opera.

The first of these was to turn spoken dialogue, which was always part of a performance at the Comique, into melodrama—that is to say, he often has his characters speak over an orchestral accompaniment. Mozart had experimented with this in his *Zaide,* as had Beethoven, powerfully, in *Fidelio.* But they had allowed, in those works, long stretches of speech with no music, and the effect of the passages where words were spoken over music was partly lost. Massenet provides virtually continuous music, so that when the characters stop singing and begin to speak intimately over the familiar melodies, when a solo violin underscores the spoken words at the lovers' first meeting, and distills the essence of those words, the effect is extraordinary. A composer who values consistency of texture will know instinctively that, if his characters are going to shift from speech to song, he has to keep that song relatively close to speech.

Massenet's second contribution to French opera is what we might call *la phrase Massenétique*—the Massenet phrase, a kind of foreshortening in the melody, a calculated imbalance that makes the musical line irregular, hesitant, tentative, close to conversation. Gounod had already scaled down French operatic singing from its grand-opera heroics in *Faust,* where one of the most effective moments is the intimate little conversation for Faust and Marguerite when they first encounter each other on the street. Massenet reduces the scale still further. For the scene at Saint-Sulpice, he crafts a melody that a lesser composer could easily work up along four-square lines to a passionate but obvious aria. Massenet keeps it conversational:

N'est-ce plus ma main que cet-te main pres - se? N'est-ce plus ma voix? _

The melody expands and contracts as Manon's feelings do in conversation. It is shaped to tell us how she feels—the physical press of the hand, the rising hope, the sudden, almost apologetic but also seductive tenderness. Prévost's original novel was naturalistic, and everyone at the time exclaimed over its psychological realism; Massenet's copy, done in these *phrases Massenétiques,* is similarly naturalistic, and often psychologically probing.

That brings us to Massenet's third contribution, his discreet use of—*mon Dieu!*—leitmotifs, recurrent phrases, as in Wagner. Massenet's compatriots were not at all happy about this "Germanizing," and his enemies, who had referred to him before as "the daughter of Gounod," started to call him, after *Manon,* "Mademoiselle Wagner." Of course, Massenet's motifs are not nearly so extensively developed as Wagner's, and they are never sounded in combination. They nonetheless pervade the opera. "The whole work," Massenet wrote, "moves and develops upon some fifteen motifs." Actually, the number can be extended to almost thirty.

The motifs are shaped by an extraordinary visual sense. The Cours-la-Reine theme that opens the opera is instantly evocative of the place, the period, and somehow of the novelettish quality of the drama to follow. The motif that begins the scene at the Hôtel de Transylvanie just as quickly calls up the frenzied and corrupt milieu of the place, and even something of the impending threat of exposure there. Des Grieux's broad cello motif admirably suggests the young nobleman with fine manners:

And Manon herself may be said to have a different motif in each of the six scenes. She is an ingenue at Amiens:

a playful homebody on the Rue Vivienne:

a courtesan at the Cours-la-Reine:

a seductress at Saint-Sulpice:

an "astonishing Sphinx, a veritable Siren" (that is what Des Grieux calls her) at the Transylvanie:

and finally a pathetic prisoner on the road to Le Havre:

Was ever a Wagner heroine so lavishly motiffed? The fifth of those themes actually sounds like Sieglinde's "Du bist der Lenz" in *Die Walküre*. And Massenet can use his motifs psychologically, as Wagner had done, to tell the truth in the orchestra when the characters on stage suppress their true feelings. When in Act II Manon tries to stop Des Grieux from opening the door of their little room, knowing that his abductors await him, she says, "Don't open that door. I want to stay with you." And she really means what she says. But Massenet's orchestra knows more. It knows what else she wants, and, as she hesitates before doing wrong, it plays over and over the motif of De Brétigny, Manon's new admirer, who has promised her wealth:

That suppressed desire has the final word. The theme surfaces climactically at the end of the scene, when Des Grieux is dragged away, and Manon chooses De Brétigny.

The Abbé Prévost wrote his novel *Manon Lescaut* as a cautionary tale: the wages of sin is death. And so I'll close these remarks with some details from three cautionary death scenes. First, from the novel. It's a little gruesome. Des Grieux lies alongside Manon's corpse on the Louisiana sands for a full day, and buries her only when he fears the attack of wild beasts. He digs the grave with his bare hands, wraps the body in his own clothes, covers it with earth after a long vigil, and then awaits his own death prostrate on the grave. To the end he loves his Manon desperately.

Then, the novelist's death. The Abbé Prévost, after a life even more picaresque and vacillating than his hero's, collapsed from an attack of apoplexy at a roadside cross—appropriately enough, for he was a failed priest. Carried to the doctor and presumed dead, he was subjected to what was thought a post-mortem examination, and actually died not from the apoplexy but under the knife. So perhaps his death, more even than the cautionary tale he wrote, was a sermon on the wages of sin.

And that brings us back to Massenet's mother, her moral strictures, and the notebook she gave him. When the little boy was grown old, and regarded as the most successful opera composer of his day, he wittily appended some "posthumous thoughts" to his memoirs. He imagined our third death scene. He imagined he was dead, and sainted, and he wrote: "I have taken up life here amid the stars. Oh, the splendor, the sparkle! I was never able to get such lighting effects for my scenes at the Opéra."

Meanwhile he can hear what the mourners are saying at his funeral. "I loved him so much," says a beautiful soprano. "I always had such success in his operas!"

"Well, now that he's dead," says a rival, "they won't play his stuff so often, will they?"

And Massenet concludes, "I knew that once the stone was sealed I'd be forgotten in a few hours."

Well, a hundred years have passed since Massenet wrote *Manon* and, if he's still looking down from the stars, he knows that the Paris that destroyed Manon has kept *Manon* alive. His chef d'oeuvre has had more than two thousand performances at the Opéra-Comique alone, and on the world's stages it still keeps company with the greatest masterpieces of the lyric the-ater. There may be other pieces that are more profound. But there are only a few—and most of those are by Frenchmen—that are so subtle.

Turandot
Courtesy Winnie Klotz, Photographer
Metropolitan Opera Association Inc.

A
CHARMING LIFE,
AND A
TERRIBLE ONE

La Bohème

A question I keep expecting to turn up on the Opera Quiz—and it's never asked—is "What do the four Bohemians buy in the shops by the Café Momus in Act II of *La Bohème?*" Can you answer it?

Well, Schaunard, the musician among the four, buys a horn with an out-of-tune D. Colline, the philosopher, buys a secondhand overcoat with big pockets for big books, and an old runic grammar to put in one of the pockets. Rodolfo, the poet, can't afford a coral necklace for his new love, Mimì, but he does buy a pretty pink bonnet to set off her nut-brown hair. And as for the fourth Bohemian, the painter Marcello—well, there's usually a trick lurking somewhere in those Opera Quiz questions. Marcello is so sick with love for his Musetta, who has deserted him, that he buys nothing. Instead, he just wants to sell his "virgin heart."

How did the impoverished Bohemians get the money for their purchases? That's an easier question to answer. They have just come into a windfall via Schaunard, who has been paid an outrageous sum by an eccentric Englishman to make music to a parrot until it died. Schaunard made music till he was blue in the face, but the bird remained supremcly indifferent to his efforts. Schaunard then decided to turn on the charm instead. He seduced the Englishman's maid—and the two of them did the parrot in with parsley. And despite Schaunard's reference to Socrates, it wasn't poison but the long stems of the parsley, which the poor bird couldn't swallow, that "done him in." (I learned that, of course, while listening one Saturday to the Opera Quiz.)

La Bohème is about much more than the four Bohemians. It is filled with music that tells of youthful love and death in an unsurpassed outpouring of melody, and that is what made it my favorite opera when I was in my teens—that and Mimì's tiny flower-hands growing warm for the last time in the muff, and the moonlight Rodolfo sees on her face when she's alive, and the sunlight he tries to shield her from when she is dead and he doesn't know it yet, and the first ray of springtime she waits all winter to see from her attic window. These, and the music that goes with them, would wring tears from a stone. But they are not all that there is in *La Bohème*. I'd like to say something here about the opera's richly detailed atmosphere, its remarkable dialogue, and especially about its four musketeers.

Puccini was well equipped to set the rakish four to music—not just because, as he said, God had touched him with his little finger and told him to write for the theater, but because he himself once lived a starving artist's bohemian life. When he was in his twenties, and poor as a churchmouse, he shared his room in Milano with an unruly baker's son named Pietro Mascagni—yes, the same Mascagni who was one day to compose *Cavalleria Rusticana*. Together they pooled their pennies to buy the score of *Parsifal,* to learn from Wagner. And together they marked the map of Milan with red crosses to show the danger areas where they might run into their creditors. There are also tales of Puccini's playing the piano fortissimo so that the landlord wouldn't hear the cooking that was going on in the room; of his carefully quartering a herring to make a meal for himself and three others; of his dining beyond his means with pretty girls at sidewalk restaurants. There is even a tale of his pawning an overcoat. Though some of these stories sound suspiciously like *post factum* biography, Mascagni himself has affirmed the truth of many of them. Together the two composers-to-be and their artist friends lived *la vie de Bohème.*

La Bohème, in recent years perhaps the most popular title in the repertories of opera houses the world over, is, curiously, a title we can't quite translate into English. Bohemia is of course part of what is now The Czech Republic, and "Bohemians" is a name western Europe once gave to Gypsies. The name seems to have been first applied to artists at the time the Church of Sacré-Coeur was built on the top of Montmartre in Paris, and colonies of aspiring, starving young artists gathered there. One such Bohemian, Henri Murger, wrote a series of short stories for a Paris newspaper on what a poor artist's life was like—"A charming life," he said, "and a terrible one": "Vie charmante et vie terrible." Murger's stories soon became a play, *La Vie de Bohème,* "Bohemian Life," and then a novel, *Scènes de la Vie de Bohème.* And that—"Scenes from Bohemian Life"—is what Puccini's shortened title *La Bohème* means.

Let's look at our four Bohemians one by one.

The tenor among the four, Rodolfo, is something of a portrait of Henri Murger himself—a headstrong, impetuous literary man, editor of a journal called *The Beaver.* Puccini characterizes him instantly as a dreamer, impatiently looking out over the smoking chimneys of Paris, his impetuous nature suggested by triplets in the musical line. In fact, Rodolfo sings most of the time in triplets, as, for example, he does in the street on Christmas Eve:

Rodolfo thinks, characteristically for a poet, in metaphors and similes. The stove that won't give warmth is for him "a gentleman of leisure who won't work for a living." As Mimì lies dying, he tells her that she is "beautiful as the dawn" and she gently corrects him, "You've got the simile wrong. You mean 'beautiful as the sunset.'" He often compares himself to a millionaire, rich with millions of dreams and rhymes. Everyone knows his great dreaming melody, the climax to "Che gelida manina," with its impetuous triplets. But what are the words to that melody? They're an extended metaphor about his imaginary riches: "Sometimes," he says, "my strong box gets robbed of all its jewels. Sometimes a pair of eyes—they just walked in with you—steal all my beautiful dreams away." No wonder he tells her, when she asks who he is, "Son un poeta." ("I am a poet.")

The baritone, Marcello, is a figure drawn from several painters Murger knew, but especially from a certain Tabar, who worked for years painting his "Crossing of the Red Sea." In Murger's stories, the "Red Sea" that Marcello paints in the attic is a picture rejected so often by the Louvre that, Murger says, if it were put on wheels, it could make the journey from the attic to the committee room and back by itself. I always feel that Puccini shortchanged his Marcello, who doesn't get an aria or even a theme of his own. But nobody ever had a better friend than Marcello, and perhaps his good heart is best seen in this strain in the duet with Rodolfo in the last act:

Schaunard, the musician without whose pluck the rest of them just might have starved, is based on an Alexandre Schanne who actually called himself Schaunard when, eventually, he published his memoirs. In the original stories, he writes rather unorthodox symphonies, one of which is called "On the Influence of Blue in the Arts"—an idea he gets when painting the blue sky from the top of Notre Dame. Yes, in Murger he's something of a painter as well as composer. But in Puccini he's all composer. In fact, he seems to have the makings of an opera composer. "La commedia é stupenda!" he exclaims, as he watches Marcello and Musetta spar across the stage. "The comedy is stupendous—but," he observes with a dramatist's insight, "Marcello will give in. Because he wants to. The hangman's noose is just as appealing to the victim as it is to the hangman." That's the kind of ironic remark Puccini often made about himself, and I've sometimes thought that, of the four Bohemians, Schaunard comes closest to representing the opera's composer.

Closest to me, I suppose, and certainly closest to the college boys I have taught classics to over the years, is Colline, the philosopher. He knows his politics and his pawnshops, and stumbles on the stairs, and says he prefers, to a wench like Musetta, a smoking pipe and a Greek text. Actually he feels the pain of loneliness, and he quotes Horace as a defense against that pain. It must be from Colline that the others come by their lighthearted classical references—when, for example, Rodolfo speaks like Nero, and says, of the burning of his play, "It's a serious loss to the century, but Rome is in peril," or when Schaunard debates in legal Latin as to whether they should admit Mimì to their Bohemian circle. Colline is the one who waves the herring they will have to split four ways, and dubs it a dish fit for Demosthenes. (The orator Demosthenes was famous for haranguing, and the words "herring" and "harangue" sound as alike in Italian as they do in English.)

Colline is bearishly big and hirsute, which the others remind him of often enough. Murger patterned him after one of his friends, called "The Green Giant" because his overcoat, with its four big pockets named after the four main libraries of Paris, got so old it had faded from black to green. Puccini gives the hairy philosopher an aria to sing, not to any of his loves but to his overcoat before he goes off to pawn it to get medicine for the dying Mimì. That overcoat, in its quiet way, bespeaks the disillusionment of Bohemian life.

What is Bohemian life? As Marcello sings, it's a "beautiful time of false illusions. You believe, you hope, and everything looks beautiful," but "it's all illusions and utopias." Murger's twenty-three stories tell us that *la vie de Bohème* is a necessary but only preliminary stage in an artist's development. The Bohemia he wrote about is not the place on the map in central Europe but the place on the edge of bourgeois society where the prospective writer or painter or composer or thinker learns about life and love and suffering and death. It is also a place he must leave before it destroys him—not by making him freeze or starve but by arresting him in a world of dreams and hopes, of promiscuity and rebellion, until, never really learning the discipline needed to write his poem or paint his picture, he despairs.

What happens to our four bohemian musketeers after Mimì dies? Well, on Murger's last page, they leave *la vie de Bohème* and, for better or worse, join the establishment. Some of them turn out, by their bohemian standards, to be failures: Schaunard writes popular songs and (perish the thought!) makes money, and Colline (even worse!) marries into high society and eats cake. Marcello gets his paintings displayed in an exhibition and actually sells one of them—ironically for Marcello, to an Englishman whose mistress is the very Musetta he had once loved. And Rodolfo gets good reviews for his first book, and Marcello tells him, "We are done for, old buddy. We are dead and buried." There is nothing left for the two of them but to settle down, sadder but wiser, to steady work, with Mimì and Musetta as beautiful memories.

Those who prefer *La Traviata* to *La Bohème* often say that Verdi's consumptive heroine rises to meet her death with tragic nobility, while Puccini's is only pathetic. But surely Mimì's death has its larger meaning, too. It is *la vie de Bohème* cruelly but clearly teaching the four aspiring bohemians what they must know in order to create. So maybe the loveliest touch in Puccini is how, after wringing our hearts with Mimì's unforgettable death scene, he ends his opera with an orchestral reminiscence of something that quietly symbolizes the opera's real theme: the artist's life, the sacrifices an artist makes, and the humanity he learns as he lives *la Bohème*. The last measures of the opera are given over, surprisingly but rightly, to Colline's overcoat:

That's *la vie de Bohème.* A life with books and art and music, filled with good fellowship and young love, but sometimes too a life cold and cruel. *Vie charmante et vie terrible:* a charming life, and a terrible one.

THE
MATURING MALE
AND THE
VORACIOUS
VIRAGO

Turandot

In the largely male mythology that has developed in the Western world over the past three millennia, the voracious virago, the destructive female that lures males to their deaths, is an archetypal figure. She is familiar from the Sirens in Homer's *Odyssey* to rose-bedded Pyrrha in the Odes of Horace to the "Belle Dame sans merci" of John Keats to the dream figures of the Freudians and Jungians of our century, who say that all of us males are afraid of her—deep in our psyches, where she lives. It is our mandate, they say, to win her, to defeat her destructive potential, if we are ever to relate maturely to the world she commands, our inner world.

In the art and the myths of intuitive males, she keeps surfacing and resurfacing, often with the mythic number three: now as the mysterious Sphinx, waylaying travelers with her threefold riddle of what it is to be a man; now as the athletic Atalanta, challenging her suitors to race with her at the risk of death, and undone finally by three golden apples; now as the

189

prudent Portia in Shakespeare's *The Merchant of Venice,* forbidding her would-be wooers from ever marrying if they cannot solve the riddle of her three (note the word) caskets.

But it is in that most mythic of art forms, opera, that this figure really comes into her own—as Turandot, Puccini's suitor-slaughtering princess, with her three mystifying questions. When the curtain sweeps upward on Puccini's opera, we see the walls of old Peking surmounted by the heads of Turandot's former suitors, impaled on spikes. And the orchestra slashes out a head-chopping chord, over and over:

Giacomo Puccini, *Turandot*

That not-inappropriately-named critic, Spike Hughes, says that that chord is as much Puccini's personal property as the first chord in *Tristan* is Wagner's. Superimposing C-sharp major on D minor, Puccini's bitonal chord seems instantly to evoke a special world, the psychic world in which the opera takes place. This will not be the charming fairytale Peking of the original play, *Turandotte,* by Carlo Gozzi. Nor will this be what we have always expected of Puccini in the past: *verismo,* his customary realistic stage illustration of some picturesque locale in Paris or Rome or Nagasaki. This time, like Wagner, and like those Italians who invented opera three centuries before, Puccini will be dramatizing myth. He will be showing us nothing less, in fact, than the archetypal myth of the maturing male—the myth, recurring in almost every culture, of what Joseph Campbell called "the hero with a thousand faces." Here is Puccini's theme for the male's maturing. Appropriately, it is announced first by a distant chorus of boys:

Giacomo Puccini, *Turandot*

© Copyright 1926 by G. Ricordi & Cie.; Copyright Renewed. Reprinted by permission of Hendon Music, Inc., a Boosey & Hawkes Company, Agents for G. Ricordi & Cie.

Then it appears, in ever more mature manifestations, when the young prince's detestation of Turandot turns to desire for her; when he accepts the challenge of her and sounds the signaling gong; and, triumphantly, when he answers her three riddles rightly.

Essential to the myth of the maturing male is the father figure. Puccini's hero has not only a flesh-and-blood father in Timur but a father figure in Emperor Altoum, who encourages him to become a son to him, and gets a theme that is related, in its pentatonic outlines, to the theme of the maturing male. Also essential to the hero myth, as our mythologists and psychologists tell us, are dual and contrasting anima—that is to say, female—figures. The mythic hero must encounter the potentially destructive anima (Turandot) and the potentially creative anima (Liù). Puccini added Liù to Carlo Gozzi's original play, perhaps instinctively knowing that his mythic treatment of Gozzi needed a saving woman. Certainly he knew that the one character who had never failed him in the past would serve him here. That character was the suffering heroine.

In common with many commentators on opera, I have a problem with Puccini, and, now that we have come to Liù, I should in honesty attempt to define it—admitting, all the while, that I could be quite wrong. When he was working on

Tosca, Puccini sent one of his friends some butterfly specimens pinned to a board, with the following note:

> These butterflies may serve to give you some idea of the transient nature of poor human lives. As corpses, let them remind you that when evening comes we all must die. While I am racking my brain in the stillness of the night to bring my Roman heroine to life, I act as executioner to these poor frail creatures. My Neronic instinct surfaces and fulfills itself.

More than one listener has sensed something of Nero, or at least something of the executioner, in Puccini. It was he who added to *Manon Lescaut* the scene in which the women destined for deportation are marched in chains before the mob at Le Havre. It was he who brought the firing squad on the stage in *Tosca,* and the lynching party in *La Fanciulla del West*—they are not there in the plays on which his operas are based. It was he who introduced the executioner grinding his axe in *Turandot,* and it was he who invented the slave Liù and had her tortured before our eyes. It is often said of Puccini that he could not compose unless competing with a rival: challenging Massenet with another *Manon,* beating Leoncavallo to the draw with another *Bohème,* tricking Franchetti out of the rights to *Tosca.* But the major stimulus to composing Puccini himself confesses in that quotation about the butterflies, and in another, yet more revealing remark, made while working on *Turandot.* "I have the great weakness," he said, "of being able to compose only when my public executioners come on the scene." His creative powers quickened when he had before him a specimen of human suffering. In his seven major works, seven beautiful butterflies—his pathetic heroines—are pinned quivering beneath the examiner's glass. Six of them die.

Puccini's confessions are made with humor and humility, but they ought not to be dismissed as light remarks. They are serious, and they partially explain why this man of prodigious musical and dramatic gifts has not been accepted by critics and musicologists as an artist of the first rank: he works, to an overwhelming degree, on a single level, and with a single interest—the sentimental examination of mental and physical suffering in his heroines.

You may say, "Well, the opera stage has always trafficked in suffering heroines." But only Puccini, of the perennially performed composers, seems interested more in the suffering than in the heroine. Mozart's Constanze, threatened with tortures, sings her defiance in elaborate, proudly beautiful roulades, supported—I like to think, defended—by four solo instruments in concertante. Verdi's suffering Violetta dies on a triumphant high B-flat, and Wagner's doomed Sieglinde exits with the radiant theme that will eventually make sense of the *Ring*'s massive cycle two dramas later. The "Anges purs" of Gounod's Marguerite storms heaven, and Poulenc's Carmelites go to the scaffold singing a death-braving "Salve regina." The sufferings of all of them point beyond the pathos of their lives. By comparison, or even considered in themselves, Puccini's heroines suffer to satisfy his—and presumably our—sense of pity.

Puccini considered many more subjects than he ever realized on stage: Marie Antoinette going to the guillotine, Nancy clubbed to death by Bill Sykes, Trilby hypnotized by Svengali, Esmeralda carried off by the hunchback of Notre Dame, Ouida's deserted Bébée drowning herself after walking from Brabant to Paris and back in her wooden shoes, Conchita (a subject eventually used on the screen by Luis Buñuel) awakened to desire by a brutal beating. Richard Rodgers, in *Carousel,* had Liliom's wife ask what was the use of wondering about the pain he caused her, and Debussy, in *Pelléas,* had his Mélisande dragged by her long hair across the stage. But each composer, with his own kind of musical understatement, pointed to meanings beyond the pathetic situations. Somehow, one knows what Puccini, also interested in those subjects, would have done had he secured the rights to the original plays. The rubati, the ostinati, the tremoli, the diminished sevenths, the thick unison tuttis thundering from the orchestra—all of these would have compelled us to tears, even as they compelled us to watch.

Try as he would, Puccini could not compose without his suffering heroine, even when, in *Turandot,* he turned his attention instead to a maturing hero. And he was plagued with doubt and despair as his myth came to realization. "This infamous *Turandot,*" he said. "It terrifies me, and I shall not finish it." At one point he predicted that at the first performance someone would have to come forward and say, "At this point the Master died." And that is exactly what did happen at the premiere. Puccini could not write past the death of the suffering Liù.

Why was *Turandot* so difficult for its creator? Not, I think, because it was on a vast scale, with a chorus and an orchestra such as he had never attempted before. That was no problem for Puccini. The writing for chorus and orchestra in *Turandot* is masterly. I think the problem was that Puccini wanted, with this final opera, to deal not just with something pathetic but with something profound. With myth. Myths are made to tell what transpires in the soul. And *Turandot* may be said to reveal its creator's soul, nakedly.

Liù is, by order of Turandot, seized and bound, and her arms are twisted till she almost dies, but she will not betray her beloved. Turandot has never seen such faithfulness. "What," she asks, "has given you such courage?" "Love," says Liù. "Love," Turandot repeats, as if she had never heard the word. It is the most important word in the opera. Liù considers her sacrifice necessary if Turandot is ever to know what it means. "You will come to love him as I do," she says. "I will close my eyes so that he will win you." And instantly she seizes a dagger from one of her tormentors and sinks it into her heart. But Turandot is not moved; she only lashes with a whip the soldier whose weapon Liù had seized.

Here is where biographers hurry in to tell us, and we cannot not listen, that at their country home in Torre del Lago Puccini and his wife Elvira had a maidservant named Doria Manfredi. Puccini was notorious for his philandering, and Doria was beautiful. Elvira was sure that the two were guilty of what she called "immoral conduct." Both denied the charge. Elvira, not satisfied, broadcast the slander through the village and kept up her face-to-face insults till, after four months, Doria killed herself—quietly, swallowing three tablets of sublimate. The press treated it all sensationally. The village was outraged. An autopsy was held, and it was revealed that Doria had died a virgin. Her family sued. Puccini settled out of court, agonizing, unable to work for a year, insisting that "Elvira too deserves pity," coping, but only coping.

The biographers all see some of these tensions in the situation Puccini introduced, with Liù, into his *Turandot*. The foremost among the biographers, Mosco Carner, sees Puccini's inability to finish *Turandot* as due to the psychological block caused by the Doria affair. George Martin says, sensibly, "To define a composer entirely in terms of his subconscious distorts the picture more than to ignore the subconscious altogether." All the same, he adds that, after a hundred years of Freud, "we cannot altogether ignore the subconscious. There is no going back."

Puccini wrote no more of *Turandot* after the death of Liù. "A questo punto," said Toscanini, conducting the premiere, "il maestro è morto." "At this point, the master died." And Toscanini laid down his baton at that point. The final scene was left unperformed that first night.

Now Puccini had laid big plans for the final scene. Franco Alfano, who eventually wrote it, had twenty-three pages of sketches and eight new musical themes left by Puccini to work with. But Puccini also knew that his treatment of the myth was at this point hopelessly confused. How could the prince let Liù be tortured? Why didn't he tell his name and stop the torture? Was his passion for Turandot stronger than his compassion for Liù? And how could he let his blind father stumble off to exile without a word? What kind of barbarians are this prince and this princess? Who cares if they ever fall in love? In a stylized fable, like Gozzi's original, we would not ask such questions. But in an emotionally charged drama, like Puccini's opera, we do.

Five different endings were suggested to the composer, and none satisfied him. Eventually, he decided to do what the master of operatic myth, Wagner, had done. After contemplating five different endings for the *Ring,* Wagner let the orchestra, not the text, resolve the issue. Puccini too would turn to his orchestra. He told his librettists to stop trying to explain the story rationally. "Love," he said, "will take possession of everything, in a great orchestral peroration." But despite two years' work on, and thirty different attempts at, that orchestral peroration, the music wouldn't come to him.

It seems to me that Puccini's problem with *Turandot* was not the Doria affair but that, for the first time, he was using myth for his material. In 1924, which was well into the Freudian present, myth was increasingly seen as a demonstration of the workings of the human psyche. The old myths were seen as happening not long ago in distant places but over and over again, nightly almost, in dreams, in the human subconscious. Oedipus and the Sphinx, Odysseus and the Sirens and the many others that are figured in Prince Calaf and Turandot came to be seen as archetypes, emblems of what happens in the maturing male who, as he comes fully into his reasoning, problem-solving powers, overcomes the threatening female. And conversely, the myths told of the maturing female who, when she is awakened to the very real vulnerability of the male, yields to him. Wagner delineated all this in the awakening of Brünnhilde by Siegfried. There's also something of the Turandot story in Lohengrin's withholding from Elsa the knowledge of his name, in Sieglinde's conferring his name on Siegmund, in Parsifal's drawing tenderness from the potentially destructive Kundry when she has conferred his name on him.

Puccini was clearly on to something when he decided to expand the contours of Gozzi's light and fanciful story. He knew he was onto something, too, but he didn't have Wagner's intuitive mythic sense. The meanings of Wagner's myths have been argued for a century and will doubtless continue to be argued for some time to come—not because they are confused but because they are truly mythic, and they keep yielding meanings. Puccini was, if not out of his depth, at least out of his element in myth. The raw materials are there, but the meanings simply won't come clear. And the composer finds he cannot set his myth to music. He cannot feel his way into the new, forbidding areas the myth opened up to him.

I think the effort of it broke him.

He was also, of course, affected by cancer of the larynx. He entered a clinic in Brussels, where he was fitted with a collar of needles. Symbolically enough, seven needles. (I always think of the seven butterflies.) It was torment for him. "I am on the cross, like Jesus," he said. "I seem to have bayonets in my throat."

The terrible operation was successful in dealing with the cancer, but Puccini's heart gave way under the strain. Perhaps in this half-hour I've said too little about that heart. In the half century since it broke, millions of people, touched by the sufferings of the seven butterflies and overwhelmed by the passionate music they sing, have been convinced that the heart that broke that day in Brussels was, despite all, a great heart.

Who is to say that those millions of people are not right?

Der Rosenkavalier
Courtesy Winnie Klotz, Photographer
Metropolitan Opera Association Inc.

STRAUSS

THAT
IS WHAT FICTION
MEANS

Elektra

When I told them in Toronto that I was going to talk about Richard Strauss's *Elektra* on the Metropolitan broadcasts, what I heard was, "But I don't like *Elektra*! It's too serious" (or "too ugly," or "too depressing"). And "I don't know what it's supposed to mean." And, inevitably, "There's all that German!"

I can see the sense of some of those objections. And that's why I'm going to begin my discussion of this relentlessly serious, sometimes ugly, possibly depressing opera not with a scene between the grim Germanic Klytemnestra and the terrible Teutonic Elektra but with a scene between two not-so-ugly or depressing English ladies, a scene from *The Importance of Being*—if not serious, at least—*Earnest*. Oscar Wilde will surely have the words, if anyone has them, to defend *Elektra* from would-be objectors.

Let's drop in on Act II, scene 1. You'll remember the setting. It's summer in an old English country garden. Under a spreading yew tree the bespectacled Miss Prism, a woman of ample years, is discovered with her books. To the back, sprinkling the flowers, is the very essence of prettiness, the delicious and deliciously empty-headed Cecily.

"Cecily," calls Miss Prism. "Intellectual pleasures await you. Your German grammar is on the table. Pray open it at page fifteen."

Cecily moves slowly stage front. "But I don't like German," she says. "It isn't at all a becoming language. I know perfectly well that I look quite plain after my German lesson."

"Child," Miss Prism insists, "your guardian laid particular stress on your German, as he was leaving for town yesterday. Indeed, he always lays stress on your German when he is leaving for town."

Do you suppose Mr. Wilde is right, that there is nothing like a good dose of German to keep a nice girl from looking too pretty? Cecily certainly looks glum at the prospect, but she brightens when she hears that Miss Prism had once, in her earlier days, written a work of fiction.

"How wonderfully clever you are!" Cecily exclaims, and she adds, "I hope it did not end happily? I don't like novels that end happily. They depress me so much."

Miss Prism answers, plainly, "The good ended happily, and the bad unhappily. That is what Fiction means."

"I suppose so," says Cecily. "But it seems very unfair."

Can that be Oscar Wilde's comment on today's opera? Well, he had himself written, in one frenzied night in Paris, a fiction that confounded good and evil, called *Salomé*. But he couldn't have known that a composer named Richard Strauss was going to turn that fiction into a German opera, and then go on to compose the even more confounding, Germanic, and unpretty *Elektra*. What Wilde did know, and said prismatically through his comic characters, was that good and evil and their consequences are indeed what fiction means, but that our conventional notions about good and evil are what fiction ought, for sanity's sake, to challenge. All comedy is largely a matter of perspective, and the delicately loony characters in *The Importance of Being Earnest* provide such perspectives. Miss Prism, indeed: her remarks refract the light. Cecily, indeed: Cecilia was the saint dedicated to art and music.

And so, with those oblique reminders that shifting lights of good and evil glance through works of art, we can turn to the great, ferocious, morally ambivalent work of art that is *Elektra*. And, Germanic though it is, let's start with its Greek antecedents.

The story is fiction with at least a slight basis in fact. More than ten centuries before Christ, Mycenae was the most powerful city in the world. Its king, Agamemnon, was set to lead the Greek forces, a thousand ships, in a punitive expedition against the city of Troy. He thought that his cause was just. But before he could sail, the winds blew against him, and he was told by a portent from heaven that he would never sail till he had sacrificed his first-born daughter. Suddenly, it was as if he had no power at all. What was wrong and what was right? He made his decision. To get the favoring wind for his thousands of men, he ritually slew that one beloved daughter, Iphigeneia. Then, during his long absence at the Trojan War, his wife, Clytemnestra (to use, for the moment, the classic English spellings), determined to punish him. She took his sworn enemy, Aegisthus, as her lover. And when Agamemnon returned victorious to his city, she and her lover slew him. Clytemnestra thought that her cause was just: it was blood for blood. Aegisthus too thought that he was acting rightly; Agamemnon's father had done terrible things to his father. So Agamemnon himself fell under the axe, naked in his bath, defenseless as ever his daughter had been.

Then Clytemnestra and Aegisthus found that they had to rule Mycenae with a reign of terror. And the mother, who thought she had rightly avenged the one child, turned on her other children: She cruelly sent her young son, Orestes, away, lest he grow up to avenge his father. Her precocious daughter Electra she kept in virtual poverty in the palace—all her prettiness turned ugly, within and without. As the years passed, and the two separated children grew to maturity, the situation built inevitably toward another act of violence.

That is where Strauss's opera begins. The part of the story his opera tells was told often in classic Greece, during a holy week in March, in the stone theater on the south slope of the acropolis in Athens. And, over the years, it was told by three of the greatest dramatists known to man: Aeschylus, Sophocles, and Euripides. Each of them told the story differently because for each of them it *meant* something different.

Aeschylus made it into a trilogy as vast as Wagner's *Ring*. In fact, Wagner read Aeschylus's work continually while composing the *Ring,* exclaiming over its power. For Aeschylus, the central character in the story is the son, Orestes, and the trilogy is called, for the son, the *Oresteia*. Grown to manhood, Orestes returns to his rightful kingdom, recognizes his sister Electra among the serving women, joins her in a long vengeance duet (a good two-thirds of a Greek tragedy was sung), and then, steeled for justice, kills his mother and her lover. Orestes thinks he is acting justly, but he cracks under the strain. Pursued by the spirits that avenge blood spilt in the family, he runs for sanctuary to the god who ordered him to act as he did, the rational Apollo. But eventually it is a goddess, the intuitive Athena, who saves him, restores his sanity, and brings, out of all the evil, eventual good. In Aeschylus God, or the gods, teach man what true justice is.

In the same theater on the slope beneath the Parthenon, Sophocles too told the story. He made the daughter the central character, and named his play *Electra* for her. She was once a beautiful girl, made for love and tenderness, but the murder of her father, and the long years of waiting for her brother, have turned her savage. Sophocles is famous for his irony, and he makes us weep that ironically this fate should befall, of all people, this affectionate, sensitive young girl. To increase the irony, he adds a new character, the gentle sister Chrysothemis, to show what Electra might have been and now can never be. So, in Sophocles, when Orestes returns and recognizes his sister and kills his mother to avenge his father, it is not he but Electra who cracks under the strain. And there Sophocles ends. God, or the gods, do nothing.

You might say, "It is a story too terrible to believe." That is what the third Greek dramatist, Euripides, seems to say. He also calls his play *Electra,* but he twists the old story almost out of recognition. He shifts the sympathy away from the son and the daughter and above all condemns the gods who allow such things to happen—and perhaps condemns too the playwrights who use the squalid old myth to justify belief in their incomprehensible gods.

In their separate ways, the three Athenians address the great question of existence. There are, I should say, three possible ways to answer the question "What does life mean?" We can speak of God, or fate, or chance. That is to say, we can say that our lives are directed either by a providential power that knows and hears and understands and helps. Or by a blind power that knows and hears nothing and is inexorable and irreversible. Or—and this can be truly terrifying—by nothing, nothing at all.

Which is true? Aeschylus comes down heavily on the side of God. The idea of God slowly emerges in his *Oresteia* like light from darkness. Gradually, through his cycle of plays, we see the sense of God's saving plan for man.

Sophocles opts rather for fate. Things happen inexorably. God, if he exists, can only warn. Man is the measure of life, and most of life, for him, means suffering.

Euripides, perhaps the most modern of the three, changes his mind from play to play. If God exists, then he, or she, is evil. Or God is only a projection of our own fears and desires. Or there is no God; nothing has any meaning; all is chance.

Now we move ahead twenty-four centuries, and from Athens to Vienna. The same terrifying questions are still being raised, but in new ways. Not in theatrical rituals on religious holy days but in the dreams of patients analyzed on the couches of Dr. Freud. And Dr. Freud is tracing the old Greek fictions not to some distant time or place where they may or may not have happened but to that timeless, newly discovered place, the human subconscious, where, he says, they continue to play themselves out furiously. Suddenly, with Freud, the old myths have become profoundly true. The time is ripe for a new *Electra: Elektra.*

Perhaps because it was Sophocles who intimated long before that the myths really happened inside all of us, in dreams, it is to Sophocles, of the three Greeks, that the finest young poet in Vienna, Hugo von Hofmannsthal, turned for his new and neurotic treatment of the story. And perhaps because it was Wagner who insisted, years before Freud, that art could make the unconscious conscious, it was Wagner's musical successor, Richard Strauss, who set the new German *Elektra* to music.

And what wonderful German it is! Can any language be so ferocious? "Da pfauchte sie wie eine Katze uns an!" Can any language be so tender? "O lass deine Augen mich sehen!"

And what wonderful music it is! The music of Freudian dreams. The dead Agamemnon stalks the score from the opening measures, which thunder out the four-note theme that seems to call his name. Soon we see that he is not a father so much as a trauma: with a crown of blood and staring eyes, he rises upward through four musical octaves, crying to his daughter:

Elektra is haunted by him, an emblem of the traumatized twentieth-century psyche:

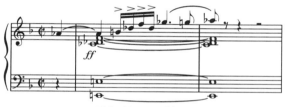

Ironically, this wounded, hate-filled girl was made for love and tenderness:

In fact, when her brother comes home, and the tension lets up, and she thinks for a moment that she won't have to hate any more, we can hear what she might have been. Her brother to her is an infant in his cradle:

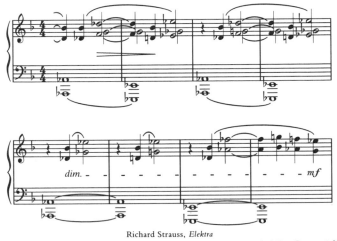

Richard Strauss, *Elektra*

But it is too late to remember the time when they were children together and had things to believe in. As her brother leaves to kill her mother, she cries through the shadows, "There are no Gods!" At the moment of the murder, she calls out, inhumanly, "Strike again!"

All these scenes are lit by torches; the figures are figures from a nightmarish dream, a Freudian dream in which, at the end, an ancient Greek choriambic rhythm wrestles with a distorted Viennese waltz. Then the orchestra ends the dream as it began it, with the traumatic cry "Agamemnon."

What does this fiction mean? I am not Miss Prism, and so I must say, frankly, "I do not know." I do not know if, with this triumph of what Elektra thinks is justice, the good ended happily and the bad unhappily. I do not even know what is good and what is evil in this story. But if I have felt my way into the work at all, I have felt, with Sophocles and Wagner and their successors Hofmannsthal and Strauss, that all of this, however repellent, corresponds to something deep in me, and that, facing it, I have been made pure. Something destructive in me has been swept away in—the famous old Greek word is *catharsis*—a great wash of pity and fear.

How wise, without knowing it, was little Cecily! It would indeed depress me if this fiction ended happily. Strangely, because it ends tragically, it leaves me feeling not depressed but exalted. That has always been the effect of great drama in the theater. At tragic performances, something of the power of God, or fate, or chance, reaches out to touch us, at a depth deeper than consciousness. We leave any of the four *Electra* plays raised to an awareness, however undefined, of the mystery of what it is to be human.

That, in the end, is what fiction means.

A
MOMENT BEYOND
TIME

Der Rosenkavalier

Creative artists often find themselves in predicaments. But there can be few predicaments so sweetly blended of exhilaration and frustration as the writer's when one of his characters grows assertive, demands a role beyond that originally conceived for him, or her, and eventually takes over the imagination of the author completely. Such a character was, for Richard Strauss and Hugo von Hofmannsthal, the Marschallin in *Der Rosenkavalier*.

The composer and librettist first conceived their opera as "thoroughly comic, as bright and obvious as a pantomime." They decided that there would be two major roles in their comedy, a "baritone buffo" and a "Cherubino": Baron Ochs and young Octavian. But as they set to work, the Marschallin, a supposedly protatic character, created merely to define Ochs and Octavian, began to take over their imaginations and their pens. She prompted the best lines and the best music. Hofmannsthal all but invented for her an aristocratic variety of Viennese to speak, and for her solo scenes Strauss scaled down

211

his vast Wagnerian orchestra to modest Mozartian proportions. What is more, in asserting her importance, this wise and gracious lady saw to it that the very nature of the work was changed as well. No longer was it to be bright and obvious. She both darkened and illumined the comedy, adding a dimension that was profound if not altogether tragic. *Der Rosenkavalier*'s theme became nothing less than the differences effected in human lives by time, with its inexorable onward flow.

The Marschallin alone among the characters sees the future passing through the present into the past, and wonders what it means. Philosophers may say that time is only the measure of change. Poets may say "Carpe diem"—"Grasp time while you can." But the Marschallin finds that in fact in a human life one cannot measure or grasp or hold. Each irreversible moment is already gone in the instant of becoming.

Most of this idea is expressed in three passages in Act I. The Marschallin is left alone on the stage for the first time. She thinks ruefully that her oaf of a cousin will get himself a pretty young bride (and a nice fortune besides), consider these as his by right, and all the time flatter himself that he is doing everyone a favor. Her mind runs back to the time, some sixteen years before, when she too—little Resi—was fetched from a convent school and sent lamblike into a loveless marriage:

Richard Strauss, *Der Rosenkavalier*

Where, the Marschallin wonders, is that little girl now? Where, she quotes as she peers into her glass, are the snows of yesteryear? She has just accused her hairdresser of making her into an old woman. Can this person she sees mirrored before her be the same that was once little Resi and before long will be "die alte Frau, die alte Marschallin"—"that old woman, the old Field Marshall's wife"? Briefly she pictures herself in that bleak future, pointed at by jostling crowds as she passes in her carriage. Little Resi's theme reappears, crusty and coarsened but still recognizable:

Richard Strauss, *Der Rosenkavalier*

Surely, the Marschallin muses, this is one of the mysteries of life—how one feels oneself always the same person, yet knows that one is constantly changing, body and soul. How can God let this happen? If he must let it happen, why has he given *her* an understanding of it? Others seem to know nothing of this. Could he not have hidden it from her? It is too much to bear. And yet, she says, in *how* one bears it, "in that 'how' lies all the difference." Here the orchestra lightly touches on the theme associated with her love for young Octavian, and hints that for her that all-important "how" somehow lies in him:

Richard Strauss, *Der Rosenkavalier*

Then Octavian bursts in on her, and in a few minutes both characters sense that, suddenly, somehow, everything between them has changed. Octavian is close, now to anger, now to tears. To convince him that it is not she who is forsaking him but he who must eventually leave her, the Marschallin sings a second little aria, and takes us to the heart of the matter, what *Der Rosenkavalier* is all about. "Time," she says, "is a strange thing. When one lives for the moment, time means nothing at all. And then, of a sudden, one is aware of nothing else. It is all around us—inside us, even! It shifts in our faces, swirls in the mirror, flows," she says to him, "in my temples. It courses between you and me—silent, as in an hour glass. Oh, often I hear it flowing, irrevocably. Often I get up in the middle of the night and make all, all the clocks, stand still."

Strauss rises quietly to this wonderful occasion with subtle orchestral equivalents for his librettist's images, and a vocal line delicately poised between aria and recitative. The Marschallin continues with a line such as had never been heard in an opera before: "But one needn't be afraid of time. It too is a creation of the Father, who created us all." How, we wonder, has she come across that Neoplatonic thought? Has her confessor given her Saint Augustine to read? Octavian understandably complains that, this morning, she is "talking like a priest." Because he is hurt and confused by the strangeness of her words, she explains that, in life, one must take what one takes lightly, "with light heart and light hands, hold and take, hold and let go." Both life and God will have it so. And we come to her third little aria, in which her resignation is complete: she will go to church, then she will visit "Uncle Greifenklau who is old and lame, and eat with him." The strings play the musical theme that at the beginning of the act was all passion, and then accompanied the observation "in the 'how' lies all the difference." Now it floats radiantly over the Marschallin's words as if to say, "This is 'how' I shall accept the inevitable changes time brings: I shall let you go. I shall confess, and perform a charitable work, and then a firm resolve will make my life new":

Richard Strauss, *Der Rosenkavalier*

Henceforth she and Octavian will be together only in public. "This afternoon," she says (addressing him, not as "you", but as "he"), "this afternoon, if I go out, and he so pleases, he will come to the Prater, and ride beside my carriage." Gentle but firm words and music of ravishing sweetness define what their changed relationship must be.

Octavian seems to understand. It is a clear case of noblesse oblige. He can be her lover no longer. He leaves quickly. Then, of a sudden, she realizes that she has seen him for the last time on intimate terms, and calls him back. Too late. He has slipped from her, like any lightly held object caught in the flux of time. When she sees him again, in Act III, he is utterly changed.

And so, through the rest of its course, is the opera. Nothing that happens through the next hours can make us forget the Marschallin. We wait, through much that is marvelous and through occasional *longueurs,* for her to reappear, to take the drama in hand and direct it to its close, for never, when she is on stage, is the music overwrought, or the dialogue spun too thin, or the drama anything less than three-dimensional.

Both Strauss and Hofmannsthal struggled to the end against the Marschallin, as if resenting the way she took over the drama and guided their pens. Strauss's comments, made years later—that she had lovers before and after Octavian, that she should not be sentimentalized, that she was "only annoyed with the hairdresser"—those remarks seem almost churlish. Surely the composer doth protest too much to be fully believed, and for almost a century now audiences have not believed him. As for the librettist, fearing for his comedy, anxious that we not feel too sorry for the Marschallin, he suggested cuts in what he called her "perilously long" scene with Octavian. But surely she is the one character in *Der Rosenkavalier* that is of a piece with his finest creations elsewhere. Again and again, in Hofmannsthal's writing, some vision of eternity brings about a moral and spiritual change in a character and enables him, or her, to survive a present crisis. Face to face with death, Hofmannsthal's famous Jedermann accepts the challenge of living, and his Ariadne accepts mythic transformation, and the husbands and wives in his *Die Frau ohne Schatten* accept their various responsibilities—all with the realization that to change is to stay alive, to stand still is to die. So here, in *Der Rosenkavalier,* the Marschallin cannot indulge her sleepless urge to wander through her darkened palace, stopping all the clocks. Time will keep moving onward, and so must she. "Our nature," Pascal says, "consists in motion. Complete rest is death."

If Strauss and Hofmannsthal were like other artists, they were themselves all too conscious of their immersion in time, and were struggling to defeat it, not by attempting to forestall the advancing years but by shaping their lives' experience into something that would never die. With *Der Rosenkavalier*, thanks largely to the Marschallin, they succeeded. It is the most enduring of their creations, and may well prove the most enduring opera of this century. So deeply has *Der Rosenkavalier* passed into our affections that Uncle Greifenklau, who is never seen and is mentioned only once, is more real to us than hundreds of characters in other operas. *Rosenkavalier*'s waltzes, which serve largely satirical purposes in their context, have taken on a noncontextual life and an identity of their own. And the Marschallin, whose Christian names are Maria Theresa, has come to symbolize Vienna itself, both the earlier Vienna of Mozart's "Dove Sono" and another Vienna with waltzes by other Strausses.

What is it that makes the Marschallin one of the great characters in opera? That she has come to symbolize Vienna, as Hans Sachs symbolizes old Nuremberg? That, like Hans Sachs, she generously renounces a love that might have filled her life anew? No, it is more than that. Just as Sachs becomes a man of stature because he comes to an awareness of human existence deeper than that of his fellow Nurembergers, so with the Marschallin: what gives her stature is her special awareness of time. At first she wishes she were not so aware, through memory, of the past, and, through expectation, of the future. But if God had denied her those, she would be, like some of the other characters in the play perhaps, one-dimensional, imprisoned in the present. *With* this awareness, she is able to come to terms with herself, and direct the comedy and the romance to their right conclusions. What enables her to adapt to change is the very thing she wished she had not been granted: the consciousness of how the past and the future impinge on the present, and, more than that, the sense of something that lies beyond time.

It is the purpose of art to show us that something does lie beyond time. Most of the action of *Der Rosenkavalier* is synchronous with clock time. But at the moment near the end when the Marschallin brings order out of chaos, when three radiant soprano voices rise in the suspended moment of "Heut' oder Morgen oder den übernächsten Tag" ("Today or tomorrow or the day after tomorrow"), a moment greater than the others has at last been reached. The action is halted, the three characters stand fixed on stage and, in the time-honored tradition of opera, the music makes its own time.

Some thoughts lie too deep for words, but not for music. The transcendent trio of *Der Rosenkavalier,* the song of three people caught up in the most important moment of their lives, assures us that this is what makes us human: we alone among creatures have a consciousness that reaches beyond the present moment. We are able to conceive, beyond time, some notion of an eternal and immutable. The still point of the turning world. When the mind reaches to that eviternity, a man, or a woman, can say to the moment, with Goethe's Faust, "Linger on, thou art so fair." In the trio of *Der Rosenkavalier* we reach such a moment—a moment beyond time. At a moment like that, when we sense what lies beyond our ordinary lives, all the clocks really are standing still.

LOVE
THAT COLORS
AND
TRANSFORMS

Die Frau ohne Schatten

How does an opera lover who knows no Freud or Jung or Joseph Campbell find a way through the labyrinth of symbols in *Die Frau ohne Schatten* (*The Woman without a Shadow*)?

One way is to see this twentieth-century opera as a variant of a much older opera everyone knows—Mozart's *Die Zauberflöte* (*The Magic Flute*). When Hugo von Hofmannsthal first broached the subject of *Die Frau,* excitedly, to Richard Strauss, he said that it would be their *Magic Flute,* much as the *Rosenkavalier* they had written was their *Marriage of Figaro.*

Hofmannsthal knew that he and Strauss could not recreate what he called Mozart's "enchanting naiveté." In *The Magic Flute* Mozart had made a childlike wonderland from the myths of many civilizations. Hofmannsthal wanted, with Strauss's music, to make a mythic universe for adults, a great symbolic drama with epic yearnings. A new *Magic Flute,* yes, but, as the librettist said, it would be a matter not of imitation but of analogy.

So, as *The Magic Flute* has two loving couples—a prince and princess, and a bird-man and bird-woman—*Die Frau ohne Schatten* also has two couples—the lordly Emperor and his Empress, and the lowborn Dyer and his wife. As the action in *The Magic Flute* is spun on by the patriarchal Sarastro, so the strange events in *Die Frau* are manipulated by the unseen but always present father, Keikobad. As *The Magic Flute* in the end consigns the matriarchal Queen of the Night to perdition, so *Die Frau* banishes a similar figure, the malignant Nurse. And as the last half of *The Magic Flute* is a series of ritualized tests for its two couples, so, with the second act of *Die Frau*, Hofmannsthal said of his two couples, "Now the testing begins, and all four must be purified."

To make his vast drama of world mythology, Hofmannsthal borrowed not just from *The Magic Flute* but, to cite only a few examples, from the Bible (the opera's characters paraphrase bits of the Gospels and the Apocalypse), from the Roman poet Ovid (the woman without a shadow has the power of metamorphosis), from the Koran (the woman with a shadow is tempted by an Efrit, a genie in the form of a young man), from the Arabian Nights (the spirits of humans sing through the fish frying in a pan), and from world folktale (the man wedded to a spirit will turn to stone if his wife does not in twelve moons bear a child).

Hofmannsthal also culled features from Omar Khayyam (who provided the character of Keikobad), from Gozzi's *Turandotte* (which contains both Keikobad and the dyer Barak), and from Goethe's *Faust* (Hofmannsthal himself remarked on the similarity between his evil Nurse and Goethe's Mephistopheles). The librettist added further symbols of his own, most notably the shadow itself. So complex did his story and symbols become that he felt the need eventually to expand and explain them in a novella. (Incredibly, only one chapter of this indispensable parergon has been translated into English—and that's a word to a wise publisher somewhere.)

The characters of *Die Frau ohne Schatten* are defined in some of the most enigmatic poetry written in this century, and in some of Strauss's most challenging music. First, there is the spirit-king who never appears but who is so important to the action that his name is announced instrumentally three times in the opera's opening measures—Keikobad.

This father-god presides over a three-part world. There is, first, the "spirit world" above the moon mountains, in which Keikobad lives with those not yet born (this pre-existence of the soul was a Platonic idea that haunted Hofmannsthal all his life). Then there is the "middle world" in which the opera begins, a kind of limbo halfway between heaven and earth, an island set in a lake surrounded by the moon mountains, where the privileged Emperor may hunt (the Hapsburgs were still in power when the opera was written). And finally there is the "earth world" far below, a place of struggling humanity, of grinding poverty and unhappiness, of passion and compassion.

From his spirit world, Keikobad predestines all that happens in the middle and lower worlds. He also, with the same seeming contradiction that besets most theologies, allows lower creatures the acts of free will that eventually save or doom them. When their crises are past, he calls them to judgment with ringing fanfares. But first he issues commands that appear fearful: he will allow his fairy daughter to learn the meaning of human love, but, if she does not find a shadow, the man she loves will be turned to stone.

Our second figure, the daughter of Keikobad, is a fairylike creature. Her mother (about whom we hear tantalizingly little) has given her a tender feeling for the lower forms of life. And so her father has let her descend to the middle world, with a talisman whereby she can assume, in sky or lake or land, any shape she pleases—bird or fish or animal. So it was as a white gazelle on the moon mountains that she was caught by the Emperor. And when she left the gazelle's body and turned again to fairy form, the Emperor loved her and made her his Empress. But then the falcon that brought them together flew off with the talisman, leaving her stranded in the interworld. She remains a spirit creature in that middle world, a woman without a shadow. As her music often suggests, light passes through her as if through rock crystal.

Strauss is famous for his operatic portraits of women. But with *Die Frau ohne Schatten* he was amazed that, for the first time, he found it easier to characterize the men in his story. Our next figure, the passionate Emperor of the South East Islands, gets the most memorable theme in the score:

Richard Strauss, *Die Frau ohne Schatten*

That ardent love is, however, without issue. The Emperor selfishly keeps his fairylike Empress far from the human race she so longs to know. And he has wounded the falcon that brought them together. A year later, the blood still drips from its wings, and it weeps as it sings to him. The Emperor cannot hear the words in the falcon's cry, the warning that if his wife does not find a shadow, he will soon turn to stone—a mythic symbol of his selfishness. But the Empress, with her spirit nature, *can* understand the song, and descends from the middle to the lower world to find the shadow that will save her Emperor.

The longest role in the opera is that of the Nurse, sent by Keikobad to accompany his daughter in her search for a shadow. A demonic figure with magic powers, the Nurse owes something to the witches and evil stepmothers of folk-lore. But she is more complex than they. Like Goethe's Mephistopheles, like Milton's Satan, she becomes the unwitting instrument of good, allowed by Keikobad to do evil so that the human race may progress toward understanding.

The search for a shadow in the lowest world brings us to our last two characters, the Dyer and his wife. He, the only character in the story who knows human love, is also the only human character with a name—Barak, a Muslim word for "saint." His occupation is important, too, though the English word "dyer" doesn't convey the full force of the German "Färber"—that is to say, "one who imparts colors." Hofmannsthal casts man on earth as a dyer in order to illustrate what is perhaps the most recurrent theme in all his poetry and prose— what he called the "allomatisches," the transformation that can be worked in any of us through the influence of another. Each of us colors the lives of those with whom we live. The saintly Barak has the power, through love, to transform. Hofmannsthal made this clear in his novella, where we see, in a vision of what a world transformed by saintliness might be, the three maimed brothers of the Dyer freed of their deformities. And Strauss, once again surprisingly more at home with his male than with his female figures, shows the transforming power of the Dyer's love by giving him a third-act aria of unparalleled eloquence, "Mir anvertraut." He chose for this his most expressive key, D-flat, the key of the trio in *Der Rosenkavalier,* of the lullaby in *Ariadne auf Naxos,* and of the violin-accompanied soprano solo, "Und die Seele unbewacht," in the *Four Last Songs.*

But even Barak needs the testing that Keikobad will send. His love has not yet transformed the most remarkable character in the opera, the one called simply the Dyer's Wife. "A strange woman," Hofmannsthal first said of her, "with a very beautiful soul, incomprehensible in her anguish, yet sympathetic." She is the flawed human figure most of us can identify with. She is what most of us *are*. Strauss gives this woman no real theme of her own. Mostly he shows her, through childlike motifs, tormented by her husband's yearning for the children she does not want, and tormented too by the voices of the unborn children themselves, crying out from the world beyond.

That brings us to the opera's central symbol, the shadow. Clearly in the narrative it signifies the ability to bear children. The shadow is the potential child in the womb. But as the opera gathers force, the shadow comes to mean something more, something close to what André Malraux called "the human condition." Suffering, vulnerability, love, guilt, death—those are what the woman without a shadow, the Empress, does not know, and wants to learn, and what the woman with a shadow, the Dyer's Wife, knows all too well, and is ready to give away.

When the crystal Empress comes to know firsthand the human condition, and to respect it, when in the last act she cries, "Ich will nicht!" ("I will not"—I will not take the shadow from that other woman if it means the loss of her humanity), then Keikobad, like all father-gods who will their children into human flesh, takes pity on her. He sends her the shadow she has earned by her selflessness. In a shaft of light it floods across the stage to touch the crystal Empress, a symbol not just of the children she will have but of her awareness of pain, guilt, death, and love—all of the things in human nature she wanted to understand, all the things the shadow means. Her Emperor, saved by her selflessness, sings, "When the crystal heart shatters in a cry, the unborn come hurrying, shining like stars"—

and we hear the voices of the children he and his wife will have.

The colorer and his wife too are united by an act of love. Her shadow, symbol of her humanity and of the children she now will willingly bear, becomes a golden arc spanning the distance between them. The final meaning of this mythic opera is stated as early as the closing measures of the first act, when three night watchmen send a song across a slumbering earth: "You husbands and wives, who lie in each other's loving arms, you are the bridge across the chasm, whereby the dead can live again. Blessed be your work of love."

I've spoken here as if it were Keikobad alone who was providentially arranging for the two couples to realize this. But in Hofmannsthal's novella it gradually becomes clear that the unborn children who live with him are a force in the drama too, at its heart, giving it meaning. In the novella the Emperor is even allowed to speak with his unborn children, three boys and a girl. By the time *Die Frau ohne Schatten* reached the stage, in 1919, it had become a poem of hope after a whole generation of young men had been lost, on both sides, in the Great War—a war in which Hofmannsthal was still young enough to be called up for military service, if not quite to the battlefield. In 1919, the hope of Europe and of the world lay in the children through whom those young dead would live again, to build the peace.

There are some who say that this symbolic opera can have no meaning today, in a world dangerously overpopulated. But *Die Frau* is not concerned with mere propagation. Its meaning is that any hope for the future rests in our children learning from us what it is to be human, and how to love one another. Hofmannsthal was, as Patrick J. Smith says in *The Tenth Muse,* "the greatest librettist of love: love as understood in its widest sense as a blend of compassion, friendship, and understanding . . . expressed at its most perfect in the marriage union between mature individuals and in the consequent creation of a family," love "with its roots . . . in the ethic of *Die Zauber-flöte.*" So, Mr. Smith notes, in Hofmannsthal's other librettos, Chrysothemis sings of the blessings of marriage and children, and the Marschallin regretfully accepts the sadness of love outside marriage, and Arabella tells her sister, "You have taught me a great lesson. That we shouldn't keep anything back, but keep giving and loving always."

Have we time, then, for one last enigmatic symbol? The falcon. At the end of Hofmannsthal's novella (required reading for a full understanding of this remarkable opera), the Dyer and his wife return to earth in a boat illuminated with all the colors of creation, and the falcon reappears to circle benignly over the Emperor and his Empress. The second or the third time you make your way through the opera, see if you agree with me that the compassionate, wounded, weeping falcon just might be, in metamorphosis, that highest of all the figures in this opera's vast mythology: Keikobad himself, leading his subjects onward to meet their destinies, Keikobad, not, as we might at first have thought, a tyrant fearful in his omnipotence but, rather, a loving father stricken with sorrow for us in the world below, weeping for us who have wounded him and must suffer so in order to find what true happiness is.

Further Reading

Because most of these studies are in print, I have cited them, wherever possible, in their recent American editions, for the convenience of the majority of those who will read this book.

GENERAL

Cambridge Opera Handbooks (New York: Cambridge University Press, 1981–). A uniformly excellent series of studies of individual operas. Each volume provides a musical analysis, a fresh appreciation, an extensive bibliography, and a discography. Julian Rushton's *Idomeneo*, James A. Hepkowski's *Otello*, Lucy Beckett's *Parsifal*, Ian Kemp's *Les Troyens*, and *La Bohème* by Arthur Groos and Roger Parker are all, in their several ways, remarkably informative and stimulating.

Nicholas John, ed., *Opera Guides* (New York: Riverrun Press, 1980–). A series of paperback volumes published in association with the English National Opera and the Royal Opera. Each volume is devoted to a single opera or composer, and contains the libretto (usually designed for singing and so only an approximation of the meaning of the original), background essays (generally excellent), musical examples, bibliography (short but reliable), discography (unannotated), and pictures (copious but poorly reproduced). At the time of writing, guides have been issued for all of the operas discussed in this volume save *Idomeneo*, *Lohengrin*, *Faust*, *Les Troyens*, *Les Contes d'Hoffmann* and *Die Frau ohne Schatten*.

George Martin, *The Opera Companion,* 3d ed. (North Pomfret: Trafalgar, 1992; originally published in 1961). Surely the best single-volume layman's introduction to opera, with informative, commonsense chapters on voices, instruments, and the byways of operatic history, and with clear, no-nonsense synopses of the standard repertory operas. (Special help is given those without much familiarity with modern languages.) Mr. Martin has also published the valuable *Companion to Twentieth-Century Opera* (North Pomfret: Trafalgar 1992; originally published in 1979), and two articulate and affectionate volumes on Verdi.

MOZART

William Mann, *The Operas of Mozart* (New York: Oxford University Press, 1982; originally published in 1977). Exhaustive but often idiosyncratic analyses of Mozart's twenty-one operas, with four interchapters on related subjects.

VERDI

Julian Budden, *The Operas of Verdi*, 3 vols. (New York: Oxford University Press, 1992; originally published 1973–1981). Comprehensive and often brilliant analyses of Verdi's nineteen operas, with five interchapters on related subjects. An immense work of much-needed scholarship that is also compulsive reading.

Mary Jane Phillips-Matz, *Verdi: A Biography* (New York: Oxford University Press, 1994). The most exhaustive and up-to-date reconstruction of the composer's life, based on more than thirty years of research in family and public archives, private libraries, and other sources. Though the author does not force her material, a new and complex Verdi emerges from this study—alternately cold and compassionate, sometimes ferocious, often depressed. Edward Rothstein says paradoxically that the book "actually succeeds in making Verdi more elaborately mysterious than he ever seemed before."

Frank Walker, *The Man Verdi* (Chicago: University of Chicago Press, 1982; originally published in 1962). The remarkable study that first challenged many long-accepted legends about the "peasant" from Le Roncole and unmade the image that Verdi, no less than Wagner, had carefully presented to the world. Philip Gossett in his introduction to the new edition rightly calls this "a detective story of the highest order."

WAGNER

Peter Burbidge and Richard Sutton, eds., *The Wagner Companion* (New York: Cambridge University Press, 1979). A remarkable collection of essays by a galaxy of Wagner scholars. Contains the brilliant and controversial piece "The Total Work of Art," by Michael Tanner (Wagner is life-affirming, and his works are a succession of related truths that make sense of the world); "Wagner's Musical Language" by Deryck Cooke (Wagner's music is, consistently from work to work, bound to the contents of the unconscious); and Lucy Beckett's "Wagner and His Critics," a humanistic overview of what Wagner meant to Berlioz, Baudelaire, Mallarmé, Lawrence, Joyce, Eliot, Nietzsche, and Mann (Wagner's achievement is both intellectual and intuitive, and "those who guess that they have something to learn from it are right").

John Deathridge and Carl Dahlhaus, *The New Grove Wagner* (New York: Norton, 1984). Such is the accelerating pace of Wagner studies that in four years the Wagner entry in *The New Grove Dictionary of Music and Musicians* was in need of wholesale overhaul. Here Deathridge and Dahlhaus take over from the earlier Curt von Westernhagen, and many commonplaces of Wagner criticism, as well as many misrepresentations perpetrated by Wagner himself in his autobiography, *Mein Leben,* bite the dust. The reader begins to feel (and he just may be right) that only now are we beginning to understand the complex phenomenon Wagner is.

Bryan Magee, *Aspects of Wagner,* 2d ed. (New York: Oxford University Press, 1988; originally published in 1968). After a quarter century, still the best short introduction to Wagner. Five pointed essays on perhaps the five most controversial aspects of the composer: his aesthetics, his anti-Semitism, his cult, his influence, and the special difficulties involved in performing his music. The writing is so clear and clean that Wagner's tortured arguments become intelligible almost for the first time. Updated in 1988 with a less-than-compelling chapter on the special importance of music among the other constituents of the *Gesamtkunstwerk.*

Barry Millington, *Wagner,* rev. ed. (Princeton: Princeton University Press, 1992; originally published in 1984). The best one-volume analysis of Wagner's life and work, both sensitive and sensible, with the up-to-date details one now misses in Ernest Newman's four volumes. In Millington's new *Wagner Compendium* (New York: Schirmer Books, 1992), many aspects of the composer's work are treated by today's Wagnerians. The quality of their contributions is consistently high.

Ernest Newman, *The Wagner Operas* (New York: Knopf, 1981; originally published as *Wagner Nights,* 1949). Long the standard volume for plot synopses cum musical examples and background detail. Any Wagnerite in good standing knows it by heart. Newman's four-volume *Life of Richard Wagner* (New York: Cambridge University Press, 1976; originally published 1933–1947) remains one of the great works of musical scholarship but lacks the revelations provided by such recently released primary biographical sources as Cosima's diaries and Wagner's own notebook, *The Brown Book*.

FRENCH OPERA

David Cairns, trans. and ed., *The Memoirs of Hector Berlioz* (London: Victor Gollancz, 1969). The best translation/edition of the best autobiography any musician has ever written. Someone ought to do the same for Gounod's *Mémoires d'un Artiste* and Massenet's *Mes Souvenirs,* both of which are charming. We are still waiting for extensive and up-to-date analyses of the operas of the two composers, and of Offenbach's as well.

PUCCINI

Mosco Carner, *Puccini: A Critical Biography,* 2d ed. (New York: Holmes and Meier, 1992; originally published in 1958). Still the standard work on the composer's life and works, this is a unique blend of intelligence, psychological perception, and good judgment.

STRAUSS

Norman Del Mar, *Richard Strauss: A Critical Commentary on his Life and Works,* 3 vols. (Ithaca: Cornell University Press, 1986; originally published 1962–1972). A first-rate work of scholarship, at once critical and sympathetic, with excellent analyses of the fifteen operas.

William Mann, *Richard Strauss: A Critical Study of the Operas* (New York: Oxford University Press, 1966; originally published in 1964). The first analysis to appear in English of all fifteen operas, and a volume to which lovers of Strauss were indebted for years. It has not been superseded by Del Mar. One wants to have both books on hand for an evening with Strauss at the turntable.

Recordings and Videos

Audio recordings are identified by their American issues on CD except in those cases where LP is the only available format. And because CD now brings performances of fifty years past to vivid new life, I shall not favor new performances with state-of-the-art sound in those cases when an older performance is clearly better from every other point of view. Video selections here are few; not every opera can be found on video in an outstanding performance or—more to the point—in a performance that one would want to see more than once.

IDOMENEO

John Eliot Gardiner's 1991 recording (DG 431674-2), with Anthony Rolfe Johnson and other singers schooled in Mozart style, and with the English Baroque Soloists playing on period instruments, is the most up-to-date (that is to say, the most authentically eighteenth-century) performance, and a very good one. If more imposing tempi, a fuller orchestra, and starrier voices (Luciano Pavarotti, Hildegard Behrens, Frederica von Stade, Ileana Cotrubas) are the desiderata, the video of a 1982 Metropolitan Opera telecast (Bel Canto 2372), conducted by James Levine and handsomely staged by Jean-Pierre Ponnelle, is an ideal choice.

RIGOLETTO

The best among many good performances remains Tullio Serafin's on Angel (CDCB 47469), with Maria Callas and Tito Gobbi ably demonstrating what all the excitement was about in 1955, but with a disappointing turn by the usually stylish Giuseppe di Stefano. For the final act alone, there never has been anything to surpass Arturo Toscanini's thrilling 1944 live broadcast from Madison Square Garden (!), with the superb singing of Zinka Milanov (Toscanini favored a dramatic soprano for Gilda), and with Jan Peerce and Leonard Warren in expert support. The CD issue (RCA 60276-2-RG) also includes Toscanini's wonderful performance of the Prologue from Boito's *Mefistofele* and the Trio from Verdi's *I Lombardi*.

SIMON BOCCANEGRA

The *Boccanegra* that the airwaves brought live from the Met on January 21, 1939, is often said to be the finest single performance in the more-than-sixty-year history of the Saturday broadcasts. The cast is astonishing: Lawrence Tibbett crowning his career as Boccanegra; Ezio Pinza facing him fearlessly as Fiesco; Leonard Warren in his debut role (and only his second appearance on the Met stage) as Paolo; and the no-longer-young but wonderfully seasoned Elisabeth Rethberg and Giovanni Martinelli as the lovers. Ettore Panizza conducts with the quiet authority that seems to have eluded subsequent conductors of the work on disc. The performance has long circulated privately but has recently been made available (on LP only) from the Metropolitan Opera, with a special donation. A CD alternative, from 1977, is Claudio Abbado's fine performance with Piero Cappuccilli, Mirella Freni, and La Scala forces, on DG 415692-2 GH2.

UN BALLO IN MASCHERA

The first Metropolitan Opera broadcast of *Ballo,* from December 14, 1940, has Zinka Milanov and Bruna Castagna in excellent voice, and the twenty-nine-year-old Jussi Bjoerling as an ideal Gustav/Riccardo—ideal except that he chooses to omit his last-act "Ma se m'è forza perderti." The performance is available (on LP only) from the Metropolitan Opera Guild, with a special donation. The 1989 Salzburg *Ballo* that was the final opera recording of Herbert von Karajan (DG 427635-2 GH2) is a sumptuous-sounding CD alternative, with Plácido Domingo in gleaming tone and a dedicated if not-quite-festival-quality cast.

DON CARLO

The five-act version (in Italian) received its best recorded performance in 1970, with Covent Garden forces superbly led by Carlo Maria Giulini (who conducted the legendary Visconti production in the same venue in 1958). On the recording (Angel CDCC-47701) Plácido Domingo and Montserrat Caballé are in glorious voice, with the rest of the cast not far behind.

AIDA

If Toscanini's intense, beautifully detailed 1949 broadcast performance on RCA (60251-2-RG) had the marvelous vocalizing that Zinka Milanov and Jussi Bjoerling provide on the 1955 recording on Victrola (6652-2-RG), there would be a definite choice here. Buy both.

OTELLO

Like all great works of art, *Otello* can be read in different ways and is, as the saying goes, greater than it can be performed. The two foremost conductors of the century have given us *Otello*s almost diametrically opposed. Arturo Toscanini's 1947 broadcast on RCA (60302-2-RG) has blazing intensity, lithe forward thrust, absolute fidelity to the composer's intentions, and a respect for the vocal line as, in the end, dominant over the orchestral. Wilhelm Furtwängler's 1951 live Salzburg performance (on Rodolphe RPC 32561.62 and other labels) has massiveness, slower textures (suggesting darker meanings), and an aural atmosphere in which the voices are set within an orchestral proscenium. Ramon Vinay is the "superb warrior" in both readings. Buy both.

DER FLIEGENDE HOLLÄNDER

It is something of a mystery that in no complete recording of this work has every element quite come together. But with each passing year, the 1955 live performance under Joseph Keilberth (on LP only—London Richmond SRS 63519), with Astrid Varnay, Hermann Uhde, Ludwig Weber, and the superb Bayreuth chorus, seems to grow in stature while rival versions come and go. A good CD alternative is the live Bayreuth performance on Melodram (MEL 26101) with Leonie Rysanek and George London, conducted by Wolfgang Sawallisch.

TANNHÄUSER

Sir Georg Solti's 1971 reading on London, with the Vienna Philharmonic (414581-2 LH3), was the first complete "Paris" version on disc, and a triumphant vindication of this work at a time when it appeared to be losing its hold on the repertory. Solti's recording would receive pride of place here, except that the Metropolitan Opera has issued an LP pressing of a stunning (if slightly cut) live broadcast from January 4, 1941, when *Tannhäuser* had as firm a grip on the repertory as anything by Verdi or Puccini. Lauritz Melchior, Kirsten Flagstad, Kerstin Thorborg, and Herbert Janssen live and breathe the characters. The young Erich Leinsdorf conducts. No wonder I fell in love with opera when I heard much the same company do *Tannhäuser* the following season! The recording, like the *Ballo* and the *Boccanegra* mentioned above, is available from the Metropolitan Opera Guild (LP only) with a special donation.

LOHENGRIN

Rudolf Kempe's radiant 1963 recording on Angel (CDCC 49017) has the Vienna Philharmonic, an Elsa (Elisabeth Grümmer) to make you believe every claim Wagner made for his heroine, a thrilling Ortrud

(Christa Ludwig), an unsurpassed Telramund (Dietrich Fischer-Dieskau), and a youthful Lohengrin (Jess Thomas) who is a little less seasoned than the others.

DIE MEISTERSINGER

No recorded performance has ever caught all of the splendors of this many-splendored work, but the reading by Eugen Jochum with the chorus and orchestra of the Deutsche Oper Berlin (DG 415278-2 GH4) is full of beautiful detail, and a century hence will be a collector's item for the unusual casting of two of this century's greatest singers—Plácido Domingo and Dietrich Fischer-Dieskau—in roles they weren't exactly born to sing but, by sheer intelligence and musicianship, make indelible impressions in. On video (Philips 070 513-3), the 1984 Bayreuth staging, rather aggressively modest, features performances (in roles they *were* born to sing) by Bernd Weikl and Hermann Prey. Horst Stein's conducting is, however, sluggish. Wolfgang Wagner makes an uncredited appearance in the closing scene.

PARSIFAL

Committed Wagnerians still argue endlessly about the relative merits of the two massive live performances directed by Hans Knappertsbusch, with the Bayreuth orchestra surging up from beneath the Schalldecke to grace the famous Wieland Wagner production in 1951 and 1962. Both are now available on CD, the earlier (with the wonderful Gurnemanz of Ludwig Weber) on Arkadia 4 CDLSMH 34035, and the latter (with the great Hans Hotter in the role) on Philips 416390-2. Beyond Bayreuth, Sir Georg Solti and Herbert von Karajan, who have made their rival ways through the Wagner oeuvre in the past three decades, achieved their most sonorous recorded performances with this final statement from the Master: Solti on London in 1972 (417143-2 LH4) and Karajan on DG in 1981 (413347-2 GH4). The choice is difficult, and will be further complicated if the Metropolitan ever issues in its special series one of the already classic James Levine broadcasts of the seventies, with Jon Vickers. To think that Wagner was worried that the world beyond Bayreuth wouldn't do justice to his stage-consecrating festival play!

FAUST

Here there is no clear choice and, given today's deplorable lack of interest in authentic French style, there is not likely to be one in the foreseeable future. Sir Thomas Beecham's 1948 reading is wonderfully piquant, but the singing of his all-French cast, while idiomatic, is decidedly uneven, and more than the standard performing cuts are made. And as the Beecham is currently unavailable on all formats, a connoisseur of *Faust* has to go back to another uneven, incomplete, but undeniably authentic recording from 1931, with Henri Busser conducting the forces of the Paris Opéra, and with two gentlemen who really believe in Gounod's masterpiece, César Vezzani (Faust) and Marcel Journet (Méphistophélès). The reissue of this performance on Legendary LRCD CD 1012-3 is more complete than that on Music Memoria 30187. A recent *Faust* from Toulouse (Angel CDCC 4228) has generally good singing, especially from Cheryl Studer, and includes as an appendix four hitherto unrecorded numbers recently discovered in the Bibliothèque Nationale.

LES TROYENS

Colin Davis's 1969 recording on Philips (416432-2 PH4), using the Covent Garden forces that gave this work its first complete performance, remains one of the events of the century, phonographically speaking: a great opera emerged from a hundred years of obscurity, and two stars ascended into the operatic firmament—Davis himself, who seemed suddenly to make sense of what had baffled others in the marathon score, and Jon Vickers, who quickly established himself as the only tenor of his time with the sound (and, on stage, the look) of a Virgilian hero. The Metropolitan's 1985 telecast, with Plácido Domingo, Jessye Norman, and Tatiana Troyanos, and with James Levine conducting, has been issued on video (Bel Canto 12509) and is often smashingly good.

LES CONTES D'HOFFMANN

Given the bewildering state of *Hoffmann* editions, simplest might, for the present, be best here. The 1990 DG recording from Radio France under Seiji Ozawa (427682-2 GH2) keeps generally to the old performing traditions and yet, with Plácido Domingo battling four different baritone villains, it nimbly suggests the kaleidoscopic nature of the piece. Domingo also appears in a video *Hoffmann* from Covent Garden (Thorn EMI 2548), and his *Hoffmann* telecast from the Met will likely appear in due time. Both are visually imaginative performances, and as rewarding musically as any *Hoffmann* on audio only.

MANON

The first choice on CD remains the longtime first choice on LP, Pierre Monteux's idiomatic 1955 performance with Victoria de los Angeles and the forces of the Opéra-Comique, on Angel CDMC-63549.

LA BOHÈME

Among many fine recordings, the standout is still Sir Thomas Beecham's perfectly paced 1956 reading, now on Angel (CDCB 47235), with luminous performances by Victoria de los Angeles, Jussi Bjoerling, and Robert Merrill. It was put together by RCA on a few days' notice in New York, a city where miracles can still happen. The 1982 Metropolitan Opera telecast (Bel Canto 2365), with James Levine conducting, and with Teresa Stratas and José Carreras as the lovers, is touching and intimate, even in the painterly but oversize Zeffirelli sets. The singing, however, often disappoints.

TURANDOT

Zubin Mehta's 1973 recording (London 414274-2 2LH2) is cast from strength, with Joan Sutherland, Monserrat Caballé, and Luciano Pavarotti (When Worlds Collide!) all in healthy vocal condition. But the Turandot of the century was certainly Birgit Nilsson, and *Turandot* fans will want to consider her five available performances, perhaps above all the 1960 recording on RCA (RCD2-5932), with Jussi Bjoerling and Renata Tebaldi, and with Erich Leinsdorf conducting.

ELEKTRA

Sir Georg Solti's 1967 recording on London (417345-2 LH2), expertly produced by John Culshaw, with the Vienna Philharmonic and the stupendous Birgit Nilsson, is unlikely ever to be challenged. Karajan's projected rival version was never made.

DER ROSENKAVALIER

It's Solti versus Karajan again. The former's 1970 reading on London (417493-2 LH3), with the Vienna Philharmonic and a surprisingly authoritative Régine Crespin, and with Luciano Pavarotti as the Italian singer, is complete and still sumptuous in sound. The latter's older 1956 recording on Angel (CDCC 49354), with the Philharmonia Orchestra and the inimitable Elisabeth Schwarzkopf, makes the standard cuts, but lovers of Strauss have with the passing years come to regard it as the classic performance. Moreover, in Salzburg in 1962, Karajan and Schwarzkopf teamed with veteran film director Paul Czinner and made a *Rosenkavalier* that is still, after a decade of operatic videos, the finest performance of any opera for the screen. The newly issued video (Kultur 1268) is, unlike previous releases, subtitled. This *Rosenkavalier* should be the cornerstone of any operatic video library.

DIE FRAU OHNE SCHATTEN

Solti's uncut 1991 performance (London 436243-2) has superb sound, generally good singing (Domingo again), and marvelous orchestral playing from the Vienna Philharmonic. There are also two fine performances with standard cuts led by Karl Böhm. Both feature the famous Empress of Leonie Rysanek, but Strauss fans will remember the earlier, pioneering performance from 1955 (London 425 981-2 LM3) with more affection because it was for most of us our introduction to the work in which love colors and transforms the world.

Broadcast Dates

The commentaries in this book were first given on the Texaco broadcasts from the Metropolitan Opera as follows:

Les Troyens	February 18, 1984
Elektra	December 15, 1984
Die Meistersinger	March 9 and 16, 1985
Lohengrin	December 28, 1985
Simon Boccanegra	March 15, 1986
Parsifal	April 12 and 19, 1986
Rigoletto	January 10, 1987
Tannhäuser	January 24, 1987
Manon	February 28, 1987
Les Contes d'Hoffmann	January 2, 1988
Otello	February 27, 1988
Aida	January 7, 1989
Die Frau ohne Schatten	December 9, 1989
Der Fliegende Holländer	December 30, 1989
Faust	March 3, 1990
Un Ballo in Maschera	January 26, 1991
La Bohème	February 23, 1991
Idomeneo	December 21, 1991
Turandot	February 1, 1992
Don Carlo	March 14, 1992
Der Rosenkavalier	February 20, 1993

Index